Neighborhood

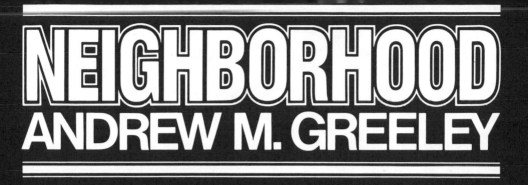

NEIGHBORHOOD
ANDREW M. GREELEY

A CONTINUUM BOOK • THE SEABURY PRESS • NEW YORK

1977
The Seabury Press
815 Second Avenue
New York, N.Y. 10017

Printed in the United States of America

Library of Congress Cataloging in Publication Data

Greeley, Andrew M   1928–   Neighborhood.
(A Continuum Book)   Bibliography: p. 173
1. Neighborhood   2. City and town life—United
States.   I. Title.
HT123.G68   301.36′3′0973   77–7119
ISBN 0–8164–9331–6

RICHARD J. DALEY

Surprised, a great city holds its breath
The harsh lake beats against an anguished shore
Black headlines scream the news of sudden death
Ink blot hero big as life—now no more.

Liberal vultures cackle on their high rise rocks
Good riddance, no one will miss the boss;
But out in the neighborhoods ethnic folks,
Both white and black, wonder and mourn their loss.

From Bridgeport, this quaint neighborhood, he came
And learned on these streets—Emerald, Halsted, Lowe,
Politics, the way the Irish play the game;
The story not yet, maybe never told
How hold a city firm, as best one can,
In the ground with the cold corpse of a man.

—Andrew M. Greeley

Contents

Introduction

Images out of your past and mine . . .
the dog across the street (a certain Sebi) . . .
the parish church . . . the school yard . . .
the corner crossing . . . the "block" . . .
It hurts to think of them for long,
so sweet are the memories.

This is a book about neighborhoods. More than that it is a passionate defense of them in word and picture against those social theorists, social planners, social policy makers, and social administrators who are bent, either intentionally or unintentionally, on destroying neighborhoods.

My defense will be neither objective nor unbiased. In some ideal order of being one could perhaps afford to be dispassionate on the subject of neighborhoods; but there are few people who are willing to suspend judgment on them and many people who are convinced that because neighborhoods are evil, reactionary, narrow, and tribal they ought to be destroyed. The overwhelming majority of our intellectual and cultural elites are not even willing to go so far as to say that at worst neighborhoods are harmless. So I proclaim my conviction that they are good and necessary things for the life of the city.

This book is not addressed to those members of the elite intelligentsia of our country whose imagery of urban life is so fixed and immutable that they are in principle unable or unwilling to consider neighborhoods as anything but "obstacles to progress," as one such person told me once. It is intended for that saving remnant who are still committed to neighborhoods and for those who grew up in neighborhoods and who, despite the pressures of the conventional wisdom, still have lurking around somewhere or other in their personalities a vague hunch that maybe neighborhood life is a good way to live and maybe the neighborhood still has a contribution to make to the solution of city problems.

As I will discuss in more detail later in the book, we approach reality with systems of "templates" or "meaning systems," fundamental assumptions around which we organize and interpret the phenomena of experience and respond to such phenomena. Our templates or our meaning systems are not merely passive receptors of empirical data; they are also shapers of reality because they influence what kind of data gets beyond the preliminary screening of our consciousness and also because in reacting and responding to our interpretations we act in the world of our physical environment and thus change its shape so that the reality we perceive after our response is not the same reality as before.

Now such systems of "basic assumptions" are not merely or even principally intellectual assumptions. Such "models" as the "melting pot," for example, or "mosaic society" are images, pictures, that exist in our emotion-laden picture-shaped preconscious. They are dense, polyvalent, multileveled symbols which perhaps correspond to intellectual propositions and from which usually the intellectual propositions are derived. To argue with a person's assumptions is extremely difficult if not impossible when the assumption is drawn from and reinforced by a powerful "picture." For many people, it seems to me, "neighborhood" is one such deeply resonant, broadly evocative picture. To try to talk about neighborhoods and ignore the vitality, the color, the emotional tug, the ambivalence, the ambiguity, the depth of feeling involved in neighborhood as image and symbol is to waste one's time entirely.

Hence this book deliberately makes use of pictures as part of its attempt to influence the reader's thinking. It begins with what I hope will be evocative recollections of past neighborhoods. I can only communicate effectively with the reader about this highly charged subject if I can activate in him some sorts of experiences of neighborhood like the ones I have had. It is not necessary that we should share completely one another's image of neighborhood; on the contrary, it is probably impossible, but it is necessary, I think, that we have had some similar experiences of small local community. The first section of the book, then, will deal with images of neighborhoods. And then we will turn to the more academic question of the origins of neighborhoods, finally discussing the future of neighborhoods.

I do not propose this book as an exercise in academic or technical social science. It is an apology in the old sense of the word, "passionate defense," of neighborhoods. However, my apology is based on, or at least grows out of, considerable amounts of social science research and theorizing on the subject which the reader is free to consult if he is interested in that sort of thing.

I should make clear from the beginning that I do not accept the distinction between "neighborhood and suburbs." Beverly, which will always be my neighborhood *par excellence,* is quasisuburban in its style. Not all suburban places become neighborhoods, and the tendency of many suburban communities to be one-class, one-age places impedes the neighborhood formation. But then not all urban places are neighborhoods either. The contention, made occasionally by Catholic intellectual types, that there are no neighborhoods in the suburbs may be true of their own suburbs or of their perception of their own suburbs, but it is by no means valid for all or even a majority of suburbs. Your neighborhood may be in either the city or the suburb.

An interesting thing has occurred in the months I have been working on the text and illustrations for this book. Neighborhoods have become "trendy." Former president Ford, who did more by his treatment of New York's financial crisis to harm cities than any president in history, appointed a commission on neighborhoods—whose recommendations are probably going to go into the same wastebasket as the reports of other presidential commissions. While the enemies of neighborhoods, whom I describe later in the book, still dominate the nation's intellectual and administrative life, they are coming under increasing attack from radical critics who in the wake of E. F. Schumacher's *Small Is Beautiful* have rediscovered localism. Some of the criticism is "radical chic," the latest stop on the seemingly endless voyage of the aging "new left"; but there are other critics, like my colleague William McCready, who are strongly committed to careful analysis of the benefits and opportunities of "neighborhood delivery systems" of social welfare programs. This emphasis is being heard more and more in the halls of some foundations and government agencies. It is too early to tell whether the rediscovery of localism is a passing fad or whether it represents a major shift in American life and culture. I am convinced that important as this trend may be, it will not substitute for sophisticated organizations made up of neighborhood citizens themselves.

Finally, I do not intend to romanticize the neighborhood. Like all forms of human community, it has its narrowness, its limitations, imperfections, failures. Some neighborhoods were richer and fuller human communities than others, and not everyone, perhaps in many cases not even a majority of those who lived in them, were really neighbors. Many of the neighborhoods of the past were immigrant entry ports, and, as we shall point out in subsequent chapters, they were often anything but pleasant places physically or psychologically. The neighborhood is not paradise; it is not heaven on earth, it is not the perfect way of human living; it is not the only form of local community that is feasible or desirable. My argument is much more modest: neighborhoods are a good thing; they make important contributions to urban life, and in their absence the city becomes dehumanized; and therefore social policy ought to cease ensuring the destruction of old neighborhoods and cease to put up obstacles to the creation of new ones. Should my argument be implemented, I think that given the nature of human nature, we would have no fear for the continuation of the neighborhood.

1

Two Neighborhoods— St. Angela's and Beverly

A back yard . . . a commuter train . . .
walking home from school . . . a symbolic corner . . .
a gothic church . . . an ancient parochial school . . .
of these things are neighborhood images made.

The strategy in this book is different from that used in most writing. I want to use images from my own past and present to stir up images from the reader's past and present. I want to appeal not only to the reader's intellect but also to his emotions and to the imagery that lurks in his imagination. For imagination to speak to imagination I must lure the reader into looking at my images—verbal and pictorial—so that they can cue responses from his store of images.

Most of my images are from Chicago. It is of the essence of neighborhoods that they be *somewhere* in a specific city. I present Chicago neighborhoods not as rivals to places like Cobble Hill or Red Hook or Polish Hill but rather as parallels. If the reader is from a neighborhood, my images are meant to stir up and reinforce his own images. These are *my* neighborhoods. Do they remind you of yours?

To emphasize this method of communicating through shared imaginings, I begin with descriptions of my two most important neighborhoods. But I will describe them almost as though they were yours, because I think you will have had experiences there very much like the ones I have had.

ST. ANGELA'S

Even when you drive down the streets on a dark, rainy March evening, the old neighborhood still has the power to stir up memories so poignant and so powerful that the years slide away in a series of sharp mental images.

> It is a hot summer day, and you are trudging down the street toward the grassy wooded playground that surrounds the tiny swimming pool. Somehow music from the Bing Crosby movie *Holiday Inn* sounds in the background.

> You're standing on the street corner of Austin Boulevard in front of the Baptist church waiting for a bus to take you downtown to the insufferably dull summer job.

> You're coming out of the smelly Follett Park gym on a cold Thursday

afternoon in midwinter with the other seminarians—cursed with a Thursday instead of a Saturday holiday—having run off vast amounts of animal energy on the basketball court.

You are sitting in the Rose Bowl, a dim ice cream parlor presided over by a suspicious-looking but attractive Greek, or waiting in line at the Jewel food store.

You are playing touch football with already badly scraped knees on the asphalt streets.

You are filing into the Catholic school in neat, orderly ranks while the sisters nervously jangle little bells. Occasionally the tall, gray-haired, beaming monsignor watches proudly.

You are looking askance at your classmates chewing garlic in preparation for driving yet another substitute teacher out of the classroom. (In sixth grade, we managed to work ourselves through six teachers in the course of a year—a real achievement.)

You are dashing to the Rockne Theater on Division Street to get there before 6:30 when the price for a triple feature goes from fifteen cents to two bits.

You are being jolted along by the rocky old red Division Street streetcars on your way to catch the Central Avenue bus to see the Chicago Bears take on the Green Bay Packers on a bright, clear October afternoon. (The Bears won in those days.)

You and your friends are poring over ship models, discussing strategies, comparing airplanes, and planning tactics to end the war. (In those days, for the very young, war was a game instead of the destructive horror it really was.)

You are kneeling in the back of church at 6:30 mass in the morning barely able to stay awake.

You and your friends meet on the school playground for softball on a Saturday afternoon.

You are studying Latin to be an altar boy.

The girls from the class are in tears on grammar school graduation day (a phenomenon which seems not to have declined appreciably in thirty-five years).

You are sitting in an old classroom with perhaps as many as sixty fellow students.

You are coming back from the seminary, encountering grammar school classmates long unseen who are, in the late 1940s, confused about whether they made the right decision not to go to college.

You are walking home from church on Sunday morning, reading the headlines about the Korean War.

You are making your first Communion in the old wooden church.

Then it is your father's funeral in the same church.

And then the memories rush in—you are saying your first mass . . . your mother's funeral . . . the new, gleaming, postwar white gothic church (with Notre Dame football players on the stained glass windows).

Time goes back even further, and the images become more jumbled, less defined: the WPA has a camp in the "prairie" (what we called vacant lots in those days) across the street from your house. The neighborhood streets are being reconstructed, and everybody jokes about how little the WPA people work—apparently they didn't understand then the connection between WPA and the battle against the Depression. You remember the Roosevelt for President posters on the side of the elevated tracks, the old open-air two-decker busses, the Century of Progress, Italo Balbo's seaplane flying over the city, the Stockyards fire, indeed the smell of the yards floating over the neighborhood on a hot, humid, stuffy, summer evening—and the yards were a long, long distance a way. You remember little children tagging along to school, having no idea how long it would take them to walk the three blocks and dashing madly those last few moments, quite certain they were late and sister would (horror of horrors!) keep them after school. And then, way, way back, you remember tricycles and Irish mails on them rushing pell mell down the sidewalk on August Boulevard, and baseball games in the alley, and horse-drawn garbage carts.

And you remember people, people you haven't seen for at least thirty years—grammar school teachers, some pleasant, others not, some saintly, some irrepressibly funny. You remember the old monsignor;

"Funeral Frank" he was called because he made every funeral in the archdiocese. You remember John Hayes, the young curate who had you doing a dialogue mass in the middle 1930s (and one hero whose feet never turned out to be made of clay). You remember your parents, far younger than they were in the last years of life, with the vitality and bounce that came back into their existence when the Great Depression was over. You remember the "prominent" parishioners (mostly, if the truth be told, insufferable dullards); you remember the kids down the street or next door, the people with whom you played basketball on the driveway in front of the garage of your house—now some of them old enough to be pastors (though not monsignors yet). You remember the best athlete in the class. (He led his team to a city championship, married the girl across the street, and even occasionally walked down the magic gridiron in the shadow of the golden dome.) You remember the smartest girl in the class, teacher's pet, a model of piety and virtue (who married a non-Catholic later on—a horrendous departure from virtue in those preecumenical days). You remember the second smartest girl in the class, who was also the prettiest, and you wonder whatever happened to her. (Looking at the grammar school pictures, she really was gorgeous. It was not just our early adolescent fantasies.) You remember the troublemakers in the class who turned out to be policemen, social workers, and politicians. You remember them all, of course, as they were thirty-five years ago, and you realize with a start that a fair number of them probably have grandchildren now.

Time goes by so fast.

You remember the precinct captain who was also the undertaker. You remember the vast numbers of fellow seminarians. For a while the parish was producing more than a priest a year, though it was not doing nearly so well with nuns. (One of your classmates is very likely to be a bishop, perhaps even before this book is published. Ironically, he would have been the troublemaker in the old days and I the company man. Well, I showed the so-and-sos!) You remember the parish saints —or at least everyone said they were. You remember the crowds in back of church on Sunday mornings. You remember the war veterans coming home in 1945 and 1946, swarming off to college determined to break out of the constraints of the Great Depression. You remember the crabs, the crazy people, the eccentrics, the haunted houses, the policemen at school crossings, the red-headed mailman, the athletic directors of the park, the courtly alderman, and even the voices of Norman Ross, Sr., and Clifton Utley on the radio at 7:55 in the morning. They all suddenly come alive again. The streets of the neighborhood are filled with memories, some of them sad, some painful, some poignant but many of them glorious.

Still, time changes. Many of the Irish have decamped from the neighborhood. Now the parish has an Italian pastor (whose days are plagued by the "helpful" and endlessly witty Irish pastor emeritus). The southern end of the parish is changing racially, the prairies have been filled by post–World War II homes, few of your friends and classmates live in the community. The neighborhood is still there though; it still seems to be able to generate loyalty among its citizens. The parochial school has almost three times as many students now as it did when you sat in its classrooms. The parish and the neighborhood may have a dubious future, but it does not seem that they will go gently into the good night.

Physically the neighborhood is your neighborhood; it is filled with your memories. But the culture, the social structure, the people have all changed. And the memories of those who have lived there more recently will have a very different tone, a very different ambience to them. There is nothing wrong with that, of course, but you still feel sorry for that which once was and isn't any more and never will be again. It's a sign you're getting old.

And as you turn off Austin Boulevard onto Augusta and head out of the old neighborhood, you remember what happened last fall when you were there taking pictures for this book. You stood near the corner across the street from the house in which your family had lived for a quarter of a century and began to take pictures of it and the children coming home from school. Behind you, filling what used to be the baseball diamond of the prairie, stood four "Georgian" two-flats. (You stood on the exact location of home plate.) Two housewives emerged from their buildings and demanded, "What are you taking pictures for?" You are taking pictures, you respond, because you like to take pictures.

"But why are you taking pictures of this neighborhood?"

"Why not take pictures of this neighborhood?"

"What right do you have to take them here?"

"Well, I want to do a book about neighborhoods, and this is one of the neighborhoods I'm interested in."

"What right do you have to be interested in our neighborhood?"

"I grew up here."

"We don't believe you."

"I grew up in that house across the street."

"We still don't believe you. Stop taking pictures here or we'll call the police."

"Lady, you go right ahead and call the police."

The two harpies returned to their houses, clearly bent on doing just that.

You have in the back seat of your car your book about St. Patrick's prayer which you carry with you on these ventures just to show people that your purposes are benign, that you are telling the truth, and that you are in fact a priest. But somehow or other you don't feel like showing this token of good intent to the two of them. You shouldn't have to do it on the very ground on which you stood for a quarter of a century.

Witches.

But what price glory? You may just be the most notorious personage the old neighborhood produced during the thirties and forties; you sneak back into it on a lovely autumn morning to take pictures to immortalize it, and they call the cops on you. The hell with them!

Childish responses, of course, but the old neighborhood calls out memories of childhood and evokes childish responses.

And then you retreat to the parish church, feeling that this encounter with the cop-calling witches is something that ought to be discussed at some length with the deity. Alas, it is high noon and the parish church is locked, as it is all the time when mass is not going on. It turns out that such is the case with most parish churches in the city, the argument being that you are protecting people that way. People praying in the church may be set upon by various types of muggers who have snuck in before them—a fear which is reasonable and valid, it turns out. So for their own good, you deprive the people of a chance to pray in the church which was built with their money—or, in this particular case, with our money twenty-five years ago. It apparently never occurred to the local clergy that one could take a leaf from other human institutions and station a watchman or a security guard in the church. One could perhaps even revive the old sacred order of porter and dress the guard in appropriate vestments. But in truth, pastors all over the city, even in less dangerous days, were never very easy with the church being open; you could watch television or play bridge with a lot more relaxed air if you knew your precious buildings were securely padlocked against all potential purveyors of mess, dirt, germs, and other human traces.

The hell with them too.

St. Angela's was a much better place, you tell yourself, in the thirties and forties, during the Depression and the war and before the advent of the affluent society.

It really wasn't. Nostalgia dims the memories of heartache, uncertainty, frustration, and smashed dreams that the Depression caused. It also dims the memory of the gold stars on the flag in the sanctuary and the funeral masses for those who were killed in action.

St. Angela's in the 1930s and 1940s was not as intensely a communal neighborhood as were many others in the city. The West Side Irish, it was said (accurately, I found out later), were much less "clannish" than the South Side Irish. (The Southsiders prefer, and still do, the word "loyal" to "clannish.") Community ties were not as tight, the Irish Catholic bond was not so strong on the West Side—perhaps because so many of them had come from Holy Family parish and were influenced by the strong assimilationist emphasis of the Jesuit fathers in that part of the city. In addition, the founding pastor of St. Angela's had been a crotchety, difficult, cantankerous person who kept to himself and did not build up much in the way of parish community. Loyalty and identification was stronger in other neighborhoods relatively close to us because the clergy had been much more self-conscious and explicit about community building.

There were Protestants in the neighborhood, of course—Baptists, Lutherans, Methodists, and Episcopalians. Some of them had summer camp meetings in tents on Division Street to which adventurous Catholic adolescents would occasionally have recourse (for disruptive purposes). What the neighborhood meant to them I didn't know and don't know. To us, though, it was the parish—not so much the ecclesiastical institution, not so much even a place of religious worship but a community of people not all of whom one knew but with whom one shared a certain fundamental loyalty and affiliation. (Though often one would be hard put to say precisely what the content of that affiliation was.) But the distinction is perhaps not valid. "Communal," "ecclesiastic," "religious"—those are artificial social science distinctions which would have made little sense to us in those days. The parish was the parish, the neighborhood was the neighborhood, the neighborhood was the parish and the parish was the neighborhood. And that was that.

If its ties of loyalty and if its activity were not as intense as one could find elsewhere, it was still a good place in which to live and grow up. St. Angela's in the thirties was a community of modest expectations— which was about all anyone could afford then. Oddly enough, for many —perhaps almost all—the expectations turned out to be far too conservative and cautious. But within those modest expectations and those take-it-for-granted loyalties, there was a serenity, a support, a self-confidence, and a set of behavior paradigms which we took for granted but which in retrospect ought not to have been at all. We were Catholics, mostly Irish but with increasing numbers of Italians; we were immigrants, the children of immigrants, and in the grammar school, the grandchildren of immigrants. It was but a decade and a half, more or less, since the restrictive immigration laws were passed, and though we didn't know it, the respectable "middle" middle class of St. Angela's was about as far as most of us had been able to get. There were some doctors, lawyers, a dentist, a wealthy police captain across the street, an occasional construction contractor whose businesses began to pick up ever so slightly in the late thirties.

Our aspirations for the future were also cautiously limited. When we graduated from grammar school in the early forties, only a few of us took it for granted we would go on to college after high school. Even in the middle forties, when the G. I. Bill caused the revolution in college expectations for the returning veterans, my own generation was at a loss as to whether to follow their example and make what seemed then the big leap forward into the upper middle class. For women, a college education was even less a matter of course; as I remember it, only three or four of my female grammar school classmates graduated from college. It was our peculiar misfortune, I would learn a couple of decades later, to have been right at the turn of the tide when the curve of national college attendance sloped upward sharply and when the curve of Catholic college attendance angled up even more sharply. (Indeed it turned so sharply that it passed the national college attendance slope within a relatively short time.) But we didn't know that then, and a lot of my classmates, I think, made decisions in the middle forties that they would regret and try to undo in subsequent years.

Still, despite the Depression and the war, there was a tranquility, a serenity, about growing up in St. Angela's at that time which would not exist among the new upper middle-class Catholics a decade and a half later. We did not realize that we were still an immigrant people; we were unaware that there was hostility toward us in the outer society. We had role models and patterns of behavior all around us; we had a church which was progressive for its time and was also friendly and benign if not frantically active; we had relatives, friends, and tight, compact social networks, which if they often restricted our vision at least provided us with the warmth and support we needed. Most of us, I think, grew up in an environment where at least we thought we knew who we were, if not personally then at least socially and culturally. It would turn out later that we were wrong and that we could revise our expectations and our ambitions upward—and for a number of us we did it with ease and considerable success. Most of us don't live at St. Angela's any more, but we look back on it with warmth and affection and with a nostalgia that is, I think, relatively free of self-deception.

St. Angela's was, I suppose, a Catholic ghetto. It was a combination of immigrant Catholicism and the counter-Reformation so enthusiastically deplored by Catholic liberals a few years later. But it didn't seem so bad then, and it doesn't seem so bad now. It was a simple, unelaborate neighborhood; it was a place to live, a place to belong to, a place to have friends, a place to grow up, a place for most people to court and to marry, a place for a few of us to have the brief day of triumph of our first mass (never dreaming how much the esteem and respect for the priesthood would erode in the years ahead with the massive resignations of the 1960s).

Nostalgia is affection with a little ambivalence mixed in. Unlike my other neighborhood, St. Angela's would not stir up much passion in those of us who left it. And I can laugh at the minor disturbance of the harpies calling the police on one of its fond citizens; it was not, after all, my neighborhood that rejected me; my neighborhood had moved on long ago, and there is a different community altogether there now —perhaps a more interesting one but one I did not understand and had never belonged to.

BEVERLY

Then there is my other neighborhood, the one whose alderman is still "mine," whose representative to Congress is still my representative (even though I haven't voted for him in more than a decade); it is still my "home" though I haven't lived there for a long time and will never live there again. It is the only neighborhood I have, and while the ambivalent feelings I have for it after twenty years are still strong and likely to remain so, I would still argue that it's the best there is.

It's a magic neighborhood.

Sometimes I think I exaggerate, but then I return to it on one of my infrequent visits and realize that the magic is still there undiminished; it is still out there in the community and not a figment of my imagination.

You drive down 102nd Street and there is your friend Nora Maeve with her notorious friend Sebastian (alias Sebi), the nicest but also the dumbest labrador in all the world. Nora Maeve waves and shouts with joy, and Sebi does what he does best, bark. He is a first-generation migrant into the neighborhood, but she is something extraordinary in any American urban neighborhood, a fourth-generation migrant. Her great grandmother lived just around the corner from where she lives now. And given a few breaks from the savings and loan associations, the Rock Island Railroad, the Chicago City Council, the dual real estate market, Nora Maeve and her brother are very likely to raise their own fifth generation in the same neighborhood.

But whence comes the magic? Is it the long line of "the ridge," the only appreciable elevation in Cook County and probably the dune line on the beaches of what was the remote ancestor of Lake Michigan? Is it the curving streets, the woods (another geological relic), the charming old turn-of-the-century homes on the east side of the parish? Or is it the new, elegant just-after-the-war homes on the west side? Is it the compact, self-contained boundaries of the community, surrounded as it is by railroad tracks, forest preserves, and golf courses? Is it the small size—not really much bigger than a small town as far as its Catholic population goes? Is it the fact that there is a history here—unlike most post–World War II Catholic suburbs? Is it that virtually everybody came to the neighborhood at the same time as part of the massive move upward of the Catholic middle class after the war? Is it that so many of the older people are childhood friends and relatives who became successful at about the same time (to their own very considerable surprise)? Is it the two modern churches in the community and the long line of progressive clergy who set traditions long before you arrived?

It is all of these things but something more, something undefinable that you will never be able to articulate even to yourself. Twenty years ago it was unquestionably a neighborhood of the new rich, and the children in the neighborhood were undoubtedly the "spoiled" children of the new rich. Even today, when wealth is no longer a surprise to the Irish and when the population composition of the community has suddenly changed, making it a much more variegated place, the new-rich atmosphere lingers—blending subtly with the artsy-craftsy environment of the immigrants from the University of Chicago area. (Few of them realize that it was within this community that the University of Chicago was founded.) Yet with few exceptions the people of this neighborhood did not act like new rich, and the children were not "spoiled." The fierce loyalty and dedication to the church, the affectionate (though sometimes supercilious) respect for the clergy seemed not to decline as the Irish moved into affluence. On the contrary it became more vigorous. God knows there was parochialism here, and it was mixed with racism on occasion; but the racists were a minority —though those who feared the crisis of a changing neighborhood were a majority (and not without some reason). The parochialism was and is sometimes staggering. Why should someone go to Harvard when they had been accepted at Notre Dame? Why read the *New York Times* when you can read the *Chicago Tribune?* How dare he write a book about us (often uttered before reading the book, of course)? Who do they think they are? But in this respect the astonishing thing was not the parochialism and the complacency that was there but that they weren't more complacent. God knows they resisted change, but when it became clear that the change was the will of the Vatican Council and not merely that of a few starry-eyed radical young curates, they enthusiastically embraced the change, and indeed left the official church behind. By their lights, they were extraordinarily good Catholics, and their lights on most occasions were brighter than those by which all too many Christians have lived. They were generous with themselves, their money, their time—amazingly generous given how recently they had arrived among the affluent. One must judge them by the opportunities that were lost, of course, but also, in main part, by the context in which they found themselves. Under such conditions, the judgment about them will not be harsh.

If there was a tragic flaw among the South Side Irish, it was not conservatism or parochialism or racism or clericalism; it was the Irish passion for respectability, a passion which, among the upper middle class and well-to-do, deprived them only of their flair and wit. Most of them could not laugh at themselves; and when the Irish cannot laugh at themselves, they've got trouble indeed.

They were great politicians and great drinkers, great story tellers and hard workers, occasionally some of them were great lovers; but they so wanted to be approved, they were so afraid of ridicule, so cautious in the face of the utterly damning, "What will people say?" or "Who do you think you are?" And if the story tellers, playwrights, and the bards, the great scholars and thinkers, the dreamers, visionaries, mystics, prophets, and saints did not grow up in that neighborhood, the ulti-mate reason was the fear of losing respectability; and it was an attitude which, sad to say, was reinforced by most of the clergy who served them. (The clerics themselves were afraid of what others would say.) If that neighborhood slips out of existence and loses the opportunity to become a permanent, stable, integrated neighborhood, the blame will not lie with the blockbusters, the redliners, the panic peddlers, or the racists; it will be the misguided passion for respectability and all its resulting caution, narrowness, and rigidity that will have destroyed the community.

But it is still alive and well. The smiling children still pour out of the schools, the ice cream parlors are filled on Saturday afternoons, gram-mar school football games keep the parks crowded all day Saturday, the crowd mill around in the back of the church on Sunday, the teenagers hang around the basketball and volleyball courts, cars speed up and down Longwood Drive, the Rock Island pulls in at 5:25, kids sneak cigarettes and beer in the park at 100th Street (maybe a little pot nowadays), volleyball games continue in the Ridge Park field house, 95th and Western traffic jams are as bad as ever, the squirrels scurry about in autumn up and down the fiery trees, sophomores still slouch aimlessly down the street on the way home from school, the bells of the church still chime for weddings and funerals (you remember the first Christmas they chimed), you can still go to Irish wakes almost any night of the week at Lynch's or Heany's or Loughlin's or Donnellen's, as one by one that old generation goes to the reward which each has both feared and expected. The precinct captains still make the city bureaucracy work for you, and children can still play on the sidewalks without fear of being harassed or hassled. The neighborhood has changed subtly; it is now almost solidly Catholic (at one time, although it seemed all Catholic, it was only half). Large numbers of city employees have moved in, clinging to the only strip on the South Side left to white people; upper middle-class blacks, even more cautious and respectable than the Irish, have joined the community; there are many more Ph.D.'s than there used to be, and a much larger number of corporate transients who will only stay for a while before moving on. (In the old days nobody ever moved out—not at least until the kids were raised.) So it is a more variegated, differentiated, and perhaps less well-integrated neighborhood. The old social controls have weakened both for weal and woe; the bonds are not as tight as they used to be. You no longer get quite the impression you once did that you are in the west of Ireland, but there are still a number of familiar faces. ("Your name is Wright, isn't it, kid?" "Yes, Father, how did you know?" "Your mother's name is Mary Ellen, isn't it?" "Yes Father, how did you know?" "Well you go home and tell her that a funny old priest asked if she remembers the day when she was your age and she got 'lost?' " The kid looks at you as though you're absolutely crazy, and you remember the astonished seventh-grader who showed up in front of her parents' house at 10:30 at night to find several squad cars and a substantial segment of the neighborhood just about ready to begin her wake. Good God, Mary Ellen, you had better not have forgotten that day, because I think it was then your husband made up his mind to marry you.)

So the third generation, and even in the case of Nora Naeve and her brother Liam, the fourth generation, is there. It is a differentiated neighborhood, perhaps a more precarious one, but still one that is so much a part of their lives that they will not give it up without a fight. More power to them, "sez" I; I only wish I were there to help.

The critical point about my second neighborhood is that it didn't have to be. St. Angela's was not an entry point for immigration; there were still a few first-generation people in the parish, and as the Italians moved in, I suspect that the number of first-generation parents and grandparents went up; but still the overwhelming majority of the people in the parish were, like my parents, second generation, the children of immigrants. St. Angela was anything but an immigrant slum; it was a respectable middle-class community. Doubtless it was still a Catholic ghetto, however, because the times were such that Catholics were predisposed to cling to one another. After all, St. Angela's came into being both physically and ecclesiastically when the restrictive immigration laws were being passed. The second generation, both by choice and by necessity, kept alive much of the ethos of the immigrant parish. In many ways the second generation were still immigrants; they were still close to the immigrant experience. They did have other options, of course, but it took special courage and special initiative to strike out on their own away from their own kind.

But by the time you got to Christ the King parish in Beverly Hills, the neighborhood was strictly optional. The people in my second neighborhood had broken out of the immigration experience economically. They no longer needed the parish-neighborhood as a community in which they could huddle together in mutual support against a basically mysterious and hostile society. The neighborhood as an entry port for immigrants and as a base of operation for the second generation was obsolescent. And yet without any hesitation, as far as one can see, the affluent third and fourth generation set about reconstructing the immigrant or second-generation parishes from the "old neighborhood" with a vigor and ingenuity that if anything made the neighborhood even more supportive, more rewarding, and a more important part of their lives. For them the neighborhood was an option, one which they both unquestioningly and enthusiastically chose.

This determination to keep the neighborhood as an important part of your life even though your economic and social circumstances do not necessitate it demonstrates the shifting role of the neighborhood in urban life. What was once an obligation now becomes an option; what was once a necessity now becomes a choice. But the option is exercised, the choice made partly because the neighborhood is magic for all those who know it (especially in my second neighborhood) and partly, too, because in the harsh impersonality of urban life it is good for there to be a place where you can be together with your own kind of people; and that is simply another way of saying that you value people who will accept you not for what you do but for who you are.

I asked myself, when I reflected upon how much these two neighborhoods mean to me, how much of what I am has come from them? It is unfashionable today to admit that one has been formed by such old-fashioned, reactionary things as neighborhoods. Those scholars who engage in theology as autobiography usually describe their development as conflict against their communities of origin, as a process of alienation, of breaking away. As G. K. Chesterton said of T. S. Eliot's "Wasteland," "I'll be damned if I ever felt that way."

I never had to break away from a neighborhood, and I don't feel alienated. If I'm not in either of my neighborhoods now, the reason has more to do with ecclesiastical tyranny than it does with personal choice. That I am a writer at all is almost entirely the result of the two neighborhoods I grew up in. Outside of my family, they are certainly the most powerful formative influences in my life. My politics, my religion, my cultural tastes, and my literary efforts simply would not be in any meaningful sense at all had it not been for those neighborhoods. My debt to both is very great indeed. What's more, I think that could be said by most people who have had similar neighborhood experiences. Only they usually are not in the position or have not the opportunity or the education to say it publicly.

"You can't go home again," a colleague at the University of Chicago told me once (restating another alienated man's assertion). He meant, I presume, that *he* couldn't go home again, and he didn't think anyone else could. But I can, I think—mostly because I never left home in the first place, and if physically I am not home, one can credit that to a vengeful cardinal rather than to any alienation. I don't know why so many of my colleagues enjoy being alienated men and women; it doesn't seem pleasant at all. Why can't you be critical of where you came from and still be sensitive and sympathetic to its strengths and assets? Why not indeed? The answer to that question tells us a lot, I think, about contemporary urban life.

2

Two Other Neighborhoods—
Bridgeport and
the Stanislowowo

The "old neighborhood" . . . fire house,
park bench, football field . . . the walk up,
the house below street level . . . the "pub" on the corner . . .
the vast old church . . . there is an "old neighborhood"
in the past of all of us who came from the immigrants . . .
even if we try to forget it. . . .

In one of the most brilliant essays ever written on the neighborhood, my sociological colleague and friend Gerald Suttles says that the neighborhood is by definition a place to be defended. The boundaries of the neighborhood are the boundaries of an important segment of one's life. One defends these boundaries because any threat to them is a threat to something that is seen as indispensable to life. Neighborhood is social turf, the place where one lives with one's family and friends; it is, Suttles suggests, that place on the checkerboard of the city where one goes, knowing that one will be "safe," where one will not have to worry about a hostile reception because one is with one's own kind. One must have, Suttles argues, in the impersonal anonymity of urban life at least some segment of the psycho-physical environment where one does not need to be on the alert for signals and cues which suggest danger, hostility, dislike, indifference, contempt.

The sociological and psychological wisdom of Suttles's position is unassailable, it seems to me, though as soon as one begins to talk about "social turf," one offends people like Martin Marty who think there is something irredeemably tribal about defending turfs (at least city turfs —suburban ones are a different matter). Those who write off as racist all those poor benighted white ethnics who are uneasy about neighborhood change simply cannot grasp how the concepts of "defended neighborhood" or "social turf" can be important to anyone. If you are worried about your neighborhood, your street, your block, your property, then by definition you are a racist—a definition usually made by someone living in a fashionable, safe, upper middle-class suburb. The intellectual and cultural elites of the country simply cannot understand that there are many people who have no objection to racial integration, no resistance to blacks as neighbors or as parents of children who go to school with your children, yet still have very powerful fears of what racial change does to a neighborhood. Neighborhood integration is fine for such people so long as it is real integration, so long as blacks and whites can share the neighborhood; but the peculiarities of redlining, panic peddling, and a dual real estate market usually mean that the integrated neighborhood is merely a transition from an all-white to an all-black neighborhood. And that in turn means that the white people who do not want to move are forced out by social and economic dynamics over which they have no control. When you have been the victim of such dynamics time after time after time, you find yourself beginning to resist. If you are sophisticated, you know that blacks are the victims of the same dynamics; they are not the cause but only the occasion of the devastation of your community. If you are not so sophisticated, you may still not object to having blacks for neighbors and still wish they would stay the hell out of your neighborhood, because when they come in you are inevitably forced to move. Even to suggest that people may think that way and not be racists is to run the risk of having yourself condemned as a racist—again by people who live in safe, comfortable upper middle-class suburbs or heavily patrolled university communities.

Some of the problems of the racially changing neighborhood—most notably soaring crime rates, increased violence, terrorism in the schools, deterioration of commercial districts—are social problems the dynamics of which we do not fully understand and about which we know relatively little. Some of the other problems—different levels of tolerance for noise in different cultures, for example, can be acutely disconcerting but are probably solvable; still others, such as ideologically reinforced racial hatred (the hatred of blacks by whites and the hatred of whites by blacks) can be controlled by effective community leadership; but the real cause of neighborhood abandonment (first by whites to blacks, then by middle-class blacks to the welfare poor) is not difficult to define or remedy: people make lots of money out of the dual real estate market, and they have enough political and economic power to continue to make it despite what their profiteering does to the life of the city. And those whose job it is to see that such profiteering does not destroy the communities of the city are normally quite uninterested —perhaps because those who are suffering the process ought to suffer. After all, they are white ethnic racists, aren't they?

Fear, violence, hatred are there when it comes time for neighborhoods to change. In the absence of such emotion, the redliners, the panic peddlers, the profiteers would not grow rich; but if the dual real estate market could be effectively policed and if integration problems could be made metropolitan and not confined to city boundaries, then the fear, the violence, the hatred would be less serious problems than they are. Many neighborhoods under those circumstances could become semipermanent, stabilized, integrated communities over the long haul. But such a solution will never be achieved until the whole of society decides that it is immoral for some people to profit on neighborhood change. It is equally immoral for other people, because of their affluence, to be able to flee from the problems of racially changing neighborhoods by moving across the legal boundaries of the city.

Part of the false mythology of urban life which justifies both the exploiters of racial change and the elites who acquiesce in such exploitation is the idea of "ethnic succession," which means (at least in the popular version) that one group succeeds another in a neighborhood. It is perfectly natural, we are told, for a neighborhood to turn black just as it had turned Italian, or Irish, or German before. It is a comfortable, convenient, reassuring way to look at the city, only it ignores the fact that one-ethnic-group neighborhoods have been relatively infrequent, and that while some neighborhoods have heavy concentrations of one group and others have heavy concentrations of another group, still most ethnic neighborhoods in the big cities have always been multiethnic. Very different, often hostile and competing groups, have shared the same neighborhood, fighting with each other perhaps inside it, but also uniting intermittently to defend it from outside attackers. St. Angela was mostly Irish but there were also lots of Germans and Italians; Beverly was only half Catholic and they were by no means all Irish; Taylor Street was Italian and Greek and Spanish and even black for a long time. Most urban neighborhoods are polyglot, and only those whose neighborhood experiences come out of the sociology textbooks think any differently.

In fact, many of the old ethnic neighborhoods have been pluralistic and polyglot for more than three quarters of a century, and have shown remarkable capacities to endure social and economic change precisely because their pluralistic structures give them great internal cohesion. Indeed, some of these neighborhoods have been able to absorb so-called minority populations in considerable numbers and still continue their pluralistic existence. I would not suggest that the advent of the new nonwhite ethnic minorities to the old neighborhoods has been always a friendly or peaceful affair, but what is impressive about these pluralistic communities is that the competition and conflict within them have been, as culture-contact situations go, relatively peaceful. White and nonwhite have slowly developed a common interest in maintaining pluralistic coexistence if not amity in *their* neighborhood.

BRIDGEPORT

Come with me for a ride through one such neighborhood, the royal borough of Bridgeport of which you have doubtless heard if you read Mike Royko's *Boss*. It is, if you choose to believe Royko, a lily-white racist neighborhood from which came Chicago's white racist Mayor Daley (who also, if you believe Royko, may have been the one to start the 1919 race riot—no evidence, of course). Be prepared for a surprise, because the Bridgeport I am taking you to see is not quite like the one Royko describes.

On the north it is bounded by the Adlai E. Stevenson Expressway, the Chicago River, the Chicago Sanitary District canal; on the east by the Dan Ryan Expressway; on the south by the Union Stockyards; and on the west by the south fork of the South Branch of the Chicago River. All in all, it is not much more than a mile square—from 25th Street at its farthest northern point to 39th Street at the southern point —fourteen blocks; and from the Dan Ryan to the south fork of the river there is at most twelve blocks and sometimes only eight. (A Chicago mile is eight blocks.) There are a couple of parks, a large quarry, and the White Sox baseball park crammed into this tiny space. Let us get off the Dan Ryan at 31st Street and drive down one of the most interesting miles in the world. And let's look at the churches as we go.

Mark well that we will never go more than two blocks north or one block south of 31st Street on our pilgrimage through Bridgeport.

We miss old All Saints Church, the "Irish" (territorial) parish at the northeastern corner of the neighborhood, because that has been torn down. But only a block off the expressway, at 30th and Wells, we find our first church, Santa Lucia–Santa Maria in Coronata, two Italian parishes combined into one. It is a tiny church and a small school squeezed into a block of two-flats, single-family buildings and an occasional apartment building. There are madonnas on the front lawns and looking out at you from the front windows on either side of Wells Street. The buildings are old but many are brightly painted, and everything on the block is scrupulously clean. Children coming out of the school are unmistakably Italian, though oddly enough, there seem to be some children with darker skins—blacks and Puerto Ricans. Did Royko see this?

We go around the block and come back down Princeton, and almost right behind Santa Maria is St. Jerome's, the Croatian parish—old church, new school—on another neat and clean street. We see another group of school children, dark- and light-skinned together. What kind of place is this?

A couple more blocks down 29th Street, across Stewart and Canal streets to Normal, and there is another church. This one is large with twin spires, elaborate trim, and a lovely facade. Two teenage black kids are walking by. "What church is that?" I ask them, a little uncertain. "That's All Saints–St. Anthony's," they reply. So the old All Saints has been merged with the German parish of St. Anthony's. These two black kids, it turns out, had graduated from the grammar school there. This is bigoted, racist Bridgeport.

The next street is Parnell, doubtless named after the Irish revolutionary, then we go by Wallace, presumably named after the Scotch revolutionary, then Lowe. You realize that a few blocks further south is the center of Bridgeport, "da Mare's" house. But today we are visiting churches not politicians. At 29th and Lowe there is the small school-church combination of St. John the Pomeson—the Bohemian church.

Mind you, you have come less than a half mile from the expressway and you have already encountered the Italian, the Croatian, the German, and the Bohemian church, as well as their schools' black, white, and Latino students. And you're not even halfway across Bridgeport yet.

The street beyond Lowe is Union; you cross 31st Street again, and there, at 32nd and Union is another small, nondescript school-church combination. (The first floor of the building is an auditorium used as a church, the second floor is the school. In some buildings, the auditorium is the basement, the first and second floors the school.) This church is St. David's, another German parish. You turn right on 32nd Street (across Halsted), suppressing a temptation to check out the 11th Ward Democratic Organization Headquarters, as well as Schaller's Pump, the bar where it is alleged that the late mayor used to do some of his drinking in days of yore (not very much, I suspect).

At 32nd and Lithuanica, one block west of Halsted, the most lovely of Bridgeport churches appears. It is the tall, slender Lithuanian church, St. George's, tucked away in a side street with a garden and a grotto and lovely old two-flats that frame what is one of Bridgeport's most spectacular pictures. And just around the corner at 32nd and Morgan, there is another spectacular church, the great big multidomed St. Mary of Perpetual Help, Bridgeport's Polish cathedral, which rivals the Polish churches in the Stanislowowo a couple of miles north (about which more later). Quite literally around the corner from St. Mary of Perpetual Help, at 32nd and Aberdeen, is Immaculate Conception, a much smaller but still charming Slovak church. You have now come just a mile from the expressway and you have seen along that mile eight churches, an average of one church for each city block. They have been Croatian, Italian, German (two of them), Bohemian, Polish, Lithuanian, and Slovak. And just two blocks further will bring you to Throop Street and the second Polish cathedral, the hexagonal-shaped St. Barbara. A right turn from there and you will be up to Archer Avenue (or Archery Road, as Finley Peter Dunne's Mr. Dooley used to call it), once the main street of Bridgeport but now huddling in the shadow of the Adlai E. Stevenson Expressway. There at 29th and Archer we end our pilgrimage at St. Bridget's, the other Irish parish. Ten blocks, ten churches—a Hapsburg Empire in miniature, with a few micks thrown in.

You have missed, however, what one might call the "procathedral" of Bridgeport—the third Irish parish at 37th and Lowe. And we all know who received communion there every morning. Within a space much smaller than a square mile, then, we encounter eleven Catholic churches, two of them Irish, two of them German, two of them Polish, one Italian, one Bohemian, one Slovak, one Croatian, and one Lithuanian. If one makes this progression, twisting back and forth across 31st Street, on an afternoon when school is letting out, one sees children of every single one of those nationalities with black and Latino children in addition. (About one-fifth of the students in Bridgeport Catholic schools are from "minority group" families.) In one neighborhood, in other words, the whole ethnic succession phenomenon is combined—and not even mentioned are the various Slovak and German evangelical and Lutheran churches which increase to twenty the number of spires you can see when you look at Bridgeport across the quarry. Perhaps this particular ethnic neighborhood might rightfully be declared some kind of national monument, a historical phenomenon of incredible pluralism in an incredibly pluralistic city and country.

If you take a self-guided tour of Bridgeport quickly you will miss the neighborhood. There are warehouses, the quarry, dilapidated business streets (particularly Archer Avenue) with very, very old store fronts. Some of the side streets that slant in from 31st toward Archer and the river have very old wooden homes—streets like Poplar, Quinn, Farrell, Elms Court are very old indeed. Some houses there probably antedate the Chicago fire and others must have gone up just after it. The entrances of these houses are on the second floor because when they were built the mud got so thick at times that entrance to the first floor was impossible. And now, because the street levels have been raised so many times, some of the little houses sit on their little plots one floor-level beneath the street. Some of these streets are dilapidated, and you see a touch of urban blight in "old" Bridgeport, but then even there many of the streets are clean and neat, the homes freshly painted.

What is in fact the core of Bridgeport, "newer" Bridgeport, Halsted to Parnell, and 31st to 39th streets, a mile long and a half mile wide? It was a neighborhood that grew up after the time of Mr. Dooley but surely before the turn of the century. It is very old indeed by Chicago standards, but shows very little sign of aging. You walk down the streets, camera in hand, and unlike St. Angela's, adults and children alike smile at you and say hello. Workmen who are busy rehabilitating the fronts of homes encourage you to take a picture now and come back later for the "after" shot.

There is public housing in the area and has been for a long, long time. (Despite what Royko and friends say to the contrary.) Inside newer Bridgeport there is no such thing as an "ethnic concentration"; the whole neighborhood is a motley of ethnic groups living side by side. Blacks do not yet go to the tiny taverns you encounter on every corner or shop in the grocery stores across the street from the tavern, but they walk the streets, apparently neither threatened nor threatening. Bridgeport didn't come by this easily. Blacks have been on the fringes of the neighborhood for more than a half century, and the 1919 race riot (one of the bloodiest in the country's history) was ignited near Bridgeport and involved many of its residents—fueled if not sparked by members of the athletic associations such as the notorious Ragan Colts. (It used to be said in those days, I am told, that if you were a Ragan Colt, you ended up either as a priest or a gangster—an exaggeration no doubt, but then Bridgeport was once a much tougher neighborhood than it is now.)

Bridgeport exists precariously—an assortment of Italians, Celts, Lithuanians, Czechs, Germans, Slovaks, and Croatians living among expressways and aging buildings that suffer from some blight; but it's still there, it's still an attractive place to live for many people who could move out of it if they wanted to. It is a conservative neighborhood, perhaps suspicious at times and certainly with its full share of prejudices and bigotries. If every part of the city had proved to be as durable as

Bridgeport, perhaps city problems would not be nearly as bad as they are. And of course it didn't hurt that the ward committeeman for twenty years was also the mayor. But all one can conclude from that is that with proper political concern, urban neighborhoods can survive, can combine most of the nationalities and the races of the urban scene in relatively peaceful coexistence if not outright friendship. And that is in itself no small achievement.

Bridgeport is a very old neighborhood, dating back to the 1830s, when Irish laborers, having worked on the Erie Canal, moved west to put in fifteen years on the Illinois-Michigan Canal. They settled in the Riverside hamlet of Hardscrabble where they raised tents first and then shanties and finally the old Chicago frame cottages. Charles Fanning, in his recent book, *Finley Peter Dunne and Mr. Dooley: The Chicago Years*, reconstructs the life of Bridgeport in the last half of the last century from the writings of Finley Peter Dunne and his immortal saloon keeper-philosopher Martin Dooley. Dooley remembered the hardships of the Atlantic crossing:

> [The widower] had been settin' on a stool, but he come over to me. "Th' storm" says I, "is over." "Yis," says he, " 'tis over." " 'Twas wild while it lasted," says I. "Ye may say so," says he. "Well, please Gawd," says I, "that it left none worse off thin us." "It blew ill f'r some an' aise f'r others," says he. "Th' babby is gone."
>
> An' so it was, Jawn, f'r all his rockin' an' singin'. An' in th' avnin' they burried it over th' side into th' sea. An' th' little man see thim do it.

And he knew the disillusionment that came with the actual employment opportunities in the new land and in Chicago:

> But, faith, whin I'd been here a week, I seen that there was nawthin' but mud undher th' pavement—I larned that be means iv a pick-axe at tin shillin's th' day—an' that though there was plenty iv goold, thim that had it were froze to it: an' I came west, still lookin' f'r mines. Th' on'y mine I sthruck at Pittsburgh was a hole f'r sewer pipe. I made it. Siven shillin's th' day. Smaller think New York, but th' livin' was cheaper, with Mon'gahela rye at five a throw, put ye'er hand around th' glass.

I was still dreamin' goold, an' I wint down to Saint Looey. Th' nearest I come to a fortune there was findin' a quarter on th' sthreet as I leaned over th' dashboard iv a car to whack th' off mule. Whin I got to Chicago, I looked around f'r th' goold mine. They was Injuns here thin. But they wasn't anny mines I cud see. They was mud to be shovelled an' dhrays to be dhruv an' beats to be walked. I chose th' dhray; f'r I was niver cut out f'r a copper, an' I'd had me fill iv excavatin'. An' I dhruv th' dhray till I wint into business.

And the memories did not go away, because in times of unrest and hardship in Chicago, many people in Bridgeport were almost as bad off as they had been in the old country.

Tis not th' min, ye mind; 'tis th' women an' childhren. Glory be to Gawd, I can scarce go out f'r a wa-alk f'r pity at seein' th' little wans settin' on th' stoops an' th' women with thim lines in th' fa-ace that I seen but wanst befure, an' that in our parish over beyant, whin th' potatoes was all kilt be th' frost an' th' oats rotted with th' dhrivin' rain. Go into wan iv th' side sthreets about supper time an' see thim, Jawn —thim women sittin' at th' windies with th' babies at their breasts an' waitin' f'r th' ol' man to come home . . . Musha, but 'tis a sound to dhrive ye'er heart cold whin a woman sobs an' th' young wans cries, an' both because there's no bread in th' house.

And life in Bridgeport was not easy even in the best of times.

Up in Archery road the streetcar wheels squeaked along the tracks and the men coming down from the rolling-mills hit themselves on their big chests and wiped their noses on their leather gloves with a peculiar back-handed stroke at which they are most adept. The little girls coming out of the bakeshops with loaves done up in brown paper under their arms had to keep a tight clutch on their thin shawls lest those garments should be caught up by the bitter wind blowing from Brighton Park way and carried down to the gashouse. The frost was so thick on the windows of Mr. Martin Dooley's shop that you could just see the crownless harp on the McCormick's Hall Parnell meeting sheet above it, and you could not see any of the pyramid of Medford rum bottles founded contemporaneously with that celebrated meeting.

After the canal opened in 1851, the Irish turned to work in the lumber yards, and, in 1865, a steel-rolling mill began operating at Archer Avenue and Ashland, just at the fringes of Bridgeport. Not too many years after that, the Union Stockyards became the hog butcher for the world. The Irish and now the German Bridgeporters went to work there, to be followed as the century wore to a close by the Bohemians, the Slovaks, the Croatians, and then the Italians, the Lithuanians, and the Poles.

The Bridgeporters were poor Irish, the shanty Irish; and when they made money they moved either south to Garfield Boulevard or west to St. Patrick's parish. They were a rough, tough, difficult lot; they fought with one another, they fought even more with outsiders; and their lives were hard. But the Irish death rate was not as high as the Polish 37 per 1,000 who lived in the Stanislowowo of the north. And Dooley could become fiercely angry at what some of the non-Irish who lived in Bridgeport suffered:

> Ye didn't know a man named Sobieski, that lived down be Grove Sthreet, did ye? Ah-ha! Well, he was not so bad, afther all. He's dead, ye know. Last week. Ye see, this here Sobieski had no more sinse thin a grasshopper. He arned enormous wages f'r a man with eight childher —wan twenty-five a day, half a week in good times, sidintary imploymint carryin' pigs iv steel at th' mills. Bimeby th' saviors iv their counthry, believin' th' market was overstocked, shut down an' left time and grocers' bills heavy on Sobieski's hands. The col' weather come on, an' Sobieski grew tired iv inaction. Also th' childher were freezin' to death. So he put a bag on his shoulder an' wint over to th' railway thracks to pick up some coal. Wan man can't pick up much coal on th' railway thracks, Hinnissy, but it is an unpardonable crime, just th' same. 'Tis far worse thin breakin' th' intherstate commerce act. Anny offense again' a railway company is high threason, but pickin' coal is so villainous that they'se no forgiveness f'r th' hidyous wretch that commits it.
>
> Sobieski walked along th' thracks, gettin' a chunk here an' there, till a watchman seen him, an' pintin' a revolver at him, called "Halt!" Sobieski didn't know th' English language very well. "Dam Pole" was

about his limit, an' hc had that thrained into him be th' foreman at th' mills. But he knew what a revolver meant, an' th' ignorant fool tur-rned an' run with his three cints' worth iv coal rattlin' at his back. Th' watchman was a good shot, an' a Pole with heavy boots is no tin-second man in a fut race. Sobieski pitched over on his face, thried to further injure th' comp'ny be pullin' up th' rails with his hands, an' thin passed to where—him bein' a Pole, an' dyin' in such a horrible sin—they'se no need iv coal iv anny kind.

"That shows wan iv th' evils iv a lack iv idyacation," Mr. Dooley continued. "If Sobieski had known th' language—"

"He'd a halted," said Mr. Hennessy.

"He wud not," said the Philosopher. "He'd niver been there at all. While th' watchman was walkin' knee-deep in snow, Sobieski'd been comfortably joltin' th' watchman's boss in a dark alley downtown. Idyacation is a gr-reat thing."

Here is what life was like for "little Tim Clancy," one of the early immigrants to Chicago's Bridgeport neighborhood.

He wor-ruks out in th' mills, tin hours a day, runnin' a wheelbarrow loaded with cindhers. He lives down beyant. Wan side iv his house is up again a brewery, an' th' other touches elbows with Twinty-Percint Murphy's flats. A few years back they found out that he didn't own on'y the front half iv th' lot, an' he can set on his back stoop an' put his feet over th' fince now. He can, faith. Whin he's indures, he breathes up th' chimbly; an' he has a wife an' eight kids. He dhraws wan twinty-five a day—whin he wurruks.

Marriage and family life in Bridgeport was not easy either.

People that can't afford it always have marrid an' always will. 'Tis on'y th' rich that don't. They niver did. That's wan reason why they're rich, too. But whin a young man is so poor that he can't afford to keep a dog an' has no more prospects thin a sound-money dimmycratic newspaper [supporting William Jennings Bryan], he finds a girl who's got less an' proposes to her an' they're married at th' expinse iv th' grocers iv the neighborhood an' they live unhappy iver after, bringin' up a large fam'ly to go an' do likewise.

But there was also fun at church carnivals and, of course, on St. Patrick's Day.

Twas a g-grand fair. They had Roddy's Hibernyun band playin' on th' corner an' th' basemint iv th' church was packed. In th' baa-ack they had a shootin' gall'ry where ye got five shots f'r tin cints. Hogan, th' milkman, was shootin' whin I wint in an' iverybody was out iv th' gall'ry. He missed eight shots an' thin he thrun two lumps iv coal at th' ta-arget an' made two bull's-eyes. He is a Tipp'rary man an' th' raison he's over here is he hit a plisman with a rock at twinty ya-ards—without sights.

I'd no more thin inthered th' fair thin who should come up but Malachi Dorsey's little girl, Dalia. "Good avnin' " she says. "Won't ye take a chanst?" she says . . . whin I come away I stood to win a doll, a rockin' chair, a picture iv th' pope done by Mary Ann O'Donoghue, a deck iv ca-ards an' a tidy [bear].

Th' booths was something iligant. Mrs. Dorsey had th' first wan where she sold mottoes an' babies' clothes. Next to hers was the ice crame lay-out, with th' Widow Lonergan in cha-arge. . . .

Acrost th' hall was th' table f'r church articles, where ye cud get "Keys iv Hevin" and "St. Thomas a Kempises" an' ros'ries. It done a poor business, they tell me, an' Miss Dolan was that sore at th' eyesther shtew thrade done be Mrs. Cassidy next dure that she come near soakin' her with th' "Life iv St. Rose iv Lima." 'Twas tur-r-rible. . . .

Displaines street . . . south to Harr'son, wist to Bloo I'land avnoo, south-wist to Twilfth, where th' procission'll counther-march befure th' Jesuit Church an' be reviewed be his grace th' archbishop, be th' clargy an' th' mayor an' th' board iv aldhermin.

Attintion! Carry ar-rms. Where's th' band? Officer Mulcahy, go over to Dochney's an' chop that band away fr'm th' bar. Hol' on there, Casey don't back that big saw horese again me. Ma, look at da-da in Gavin's hack. Ar-re ye ready? Play up th' wearin' iv th' green, ye baloon-headed Dutchmin. Hannigan, go an' get th' polis to intherfere—th' Sons iv Saint Patrick an' th' Ancient Order's come together. Glory be, me saddle's sliipin'. Ar-re ye ready? For-wa-ard march!

However rough life may have been in Bridgeport when the young Finley Peter Dunne and the saloon keeper Dooley observed it, it was much better organized and much less degrading than the conditions in New York and Boston twenty years earlier. Irish immigrants were still coming in in the 1880s, though not at such a rapid rate as in previous years. But now there was a community organized to receive them and to orient them toward the new society. One of the fascinating and as yet unresearched historical questions is how long it took each of the groups to establish a "receiving" community which could protect the newest immigrants from abject poverty and exploitation when they arrived on American shores.

There is no point in glamorizing the immigrant neighborhood. Life was difficult, but for many of the immigrants it became much less difficult than it was for them in the country they had left behind. Few of them seemed disposed to go back in any case.

The neighborhood soon became the source of power and strength. It was the immigrant's political base—tenuous and very rough, at that:

> Whin Andy Duggan r-run f'r aldherman against Schwartzmeister, th' big Dutchman,—I was precinct captain then, Jawn,—there was an iliction f'r ye. Twas on our precinct they relied to ilict Duggan; f'r th' Dutch was sthrong down be th' thrack, an' Schwartzmeister had a band out playin' "Th' Watch on th' Rhine." Well, sir, we opened th' polls at six o'clock, an' there was tin Schwartzmeister men there to protect his intherests. At sivin o'clock there was only three, an' wan iv thim was goin' up th' sthreet with Hinnissy kickin' at him. At eight o'clock, be dad, there was on' wan' an' he was sittin' on th' roof iv Gavin's blacksmith shop, an' th' la-ads was thryin' to borrow a laddher fr'm th' injine-house f'r to get at him. . . . We cast twenty-wan hundhred votes f'r Duggan, an' they was on'y five hundhred votes in th' precinct. We'd cast more, but th' tickets give out. . . .

The neighborhood also became an economic base. Craftsmen, storekeepers, undertakers, school teachers, saloon keepers like Dooley, contractors, deliverymen, the occasional doctor, lawyer, or dentist began to amass moderate and eventually substantial incomes by serving the needs of the immigrant community. You tended to do business with "your own kind."*

Williamsburg, Beacon Hill, Riverside Drive—Bridgeport is not. Its history is one of hardship, suffering, sacrifice, brutally hard work, the story of survival. The people of Bridgeport survived—at least some of them did—and their neighborhood certainly survived. Many of the families have left but enough remain; one has the impression that among the younger generation, there are far more who intend to remain. The suburban temptation for the college-educated youth of Bridgeport is not quite what it was for their predecessors twenty years ago. They probably know little of their own history; many probably never even heard of Martin Dooley. They don't know about the rolling mills and the lumber yards and the canal diggers and the fierce Atlantic crossings, the old parish socials, the strikes, the cold, militant Irish nationalism, the 1919 race riot, and the stockyards and the quarry. It's a shame they don't because they might appreciate more than they do just what they have.

And the real monument to the strength and vitality of the city of Chicago may not after all be the lost home of Mrs. Potter Palmer or the lost Garrick Theatre or the auditorium; the real monument may be the ethnic streets of Bridgeport with the firehouses, tiny taverns, neighborhood groceries, second-story entrances, below street-level yards, and their Italian, Croatian, Slovak, Bohemian, Luthuanian, Polish, Irish, German, black, and Mexican kids.

THE STANISLOWOWO

Now drive with me down the John F. Kennedy Expressway from O'Hare Airport and see the great string of Polish cathedrals that begins with St. Mary of the Angels just north of North Avenue and runs along

---

*I have barely scraped the surface with a few quotes of the extraordinarily rich portrait of Bridgeport life the last two decades of the last century that Fanning put together out of the Dooley material. It's a book not to be missed by anyone interested in urban neighborhoods.

the right-hand side of the expressway by St. Stanislaus Kostka (the protochurch of Polish "downtown," which gives its name to the whole community—thus "Stanislowowo"). Just two blocks south on Division Street is Holy Trinity, eldest daughter and principal rival of "St. Stan's." At Chicago Avenue there stands the huge St. John Kantius, whose green domes are silhouetted against the blue afternoon sky. Just a couple of blocks west is the one diocesan Polish cathedral, Holy Innocents. (The other four churches were all built by the Resurrectionist Order and antedate Holy Innocents.) All these churches are vast structures—elaborate, ornate, impressive if perhaps not exactly modern in their architectural tastes. Hardly an Irish church in the city can compare in splendor to the huge edifices that the impoverished Polish immigrants put up. A waste of money? It would seem that the clergy who built them and the laity who paid for them didn't think so. For the churches represented to the immigrant loyalty to his heritage, to his native land, to his religious faith, and to his new nation. The Polish cathedrals were acts of faith and hope; and, as it turned out, the faith was rewarded and the hope realized.

Two points must be noted about the Stanislowowo. First, while it was from the beginning a heavily Polish neighborhood (its beginning can be marked from the establishment of the St. Stanislaus Kostka Association by the Civil War cavalry officer, Peter Kiolbassa, in the late 1860s), it never was completely Polish. According to Edward Kantowicz, in his *Polish-American Politics in Chicago,* even at the height of its splendors, Polish "downtown" (the Stanislowowo) was only 47 per cent Polish (13 per cent German and 7 per cent Italian). Incidentally, Kantowicz estimates that the population of Bridgeport at the same time was 22 per cent Polish, 16 per cent German, 7 per cent Lithuanian, 7 per cent Irish, and 7 per cent Italian. (His figures represent foreign born and native born of foreign parents, presumably, so that in the Irish and German cases, the percentages are probably somewhat higher.)

There are other churches in the area. Assumption is right around the corner from St. Mary of the Angels; St. Boniface, the German parish, is on Noble Avenue (the so-called Polish corridor), within a stone's

throw of Holy Trinity and St. Stan's. Indeed it was the German parishioners of St. Boniface who made the St. Stanislaus Kostka Society
welcome before they had their own church. And in the same area you
could find St. Columbkille's, the most venerated church of the West
Side Irish parishes, Santa Maria Addolorata, (as you might guess) the
Italian parish, St. Stephan of Hungary, and St. Michael, another German parish (and the one to which my father—who was scarcely German—went to church).

The area around the Stanislowowo, then, was by no means completely Polish, though the few blocks around each of the major Polish
"cathedrals" must have been overwhelmingly so. No claim can be made
that ethnic barriers did not exist in those neighborhoods, or that all was
peace and friendliness and harmony among the various groups. There
was conflict, competition, occasional violence between the street gangs,
and not infrequent exploitation—and the Poles, as the most recent
arrivals, were the obvious victims. And yet, the ordinary and normal
situation in the Stanislowowo was moderately peaceful coexistence, as
it was in Bridgeport. Indeed there was far more conflict within the
Polish community over issues of Polish nationalism than there was
between the Poles and their non-Polish neighbors. Despite its Polish
name, the Stanislowowo was pluralistic from the beginning.*

"Westtown," "Lincoln Park," and "Logan Square," the three community areas embraced by the Polish downtown, have become in the
last two decades one of the two strongest concentrations of Puerto
Ricans and Mexicans in the Chicago area. Many of the Poles have
moved further north along Milwaukee Avenue toward the suburbs. But
some have stayed, and despite the liberal image of Poles as being
narrow, bigoted, and racist, the two populations seem to manage to live

*Some estimates suggest that while the community is now majority Hispanic, there
are still enough Poles in it to constitute two-fifths of its inhabitants. A detailed plan
for neighborhood conservation—down to details about what should be done to which
houses—is contained in a Chicago "Community 21" report, "Program for Improvement 1977–1980," available from the National Center for Urban Ethnic Affairs, 1521
16th St., N.W., Washington D.C..

together without major disturbances. Indeed, during the 1960s, on one occasion when the Latinos in the area were demonstrating against the Chicago police force, the Poles who shared the area with them went about their daily business unperturbed—and, as it turned out, also undisturbed by the Latinos, who themselves had no trouble distinguishing between the city of Chicago and their Polish neighbors. And when the Latinos began what I call "the color revolution" (about which more later) in Chicago, the Poles, always proud of the neatness of their own homes, quickly followed suit. It's hard to tell now, as you drive through the Stanislowowo, which houses are Polish and which are Latin because they are all painted brightly.

I do not wish to make a case for any great and intimate friendship between the Polish and the Latino communities. But they have managed to survive alongside one another in relative peace, occupying a neighborhood which both claim to be theirs and which both have made common cause to defend against the city and federal governments. Such militant neighborhood organizations as MAHA (Metropolitan Area Housing Alliance) bring together Poles, Latins, blacks, and anybody else in sight to tilt against not only City Hall but also Washington. Their particular cause is redlining, and so far at least they have not lost.

The Stanislowowo was written off a half century ago by the "Chicago School" of sociology as a place of acute social disorganization. The literature of that school, *Gold Coast and the Slum, The Gang,* and *The Polish Peasant in Europe and America,* were written about the Stanislowowo from that perspective. But as one drives through the community today and observes the new town houses that have been constructed and some of the old ones that have been rehabilitated, and one sees Slavic and Latin children coming out of the same parochial schools, it is astonishing that anyone could have seen social disorganization here.

Just east of the Stanislowowo, across the Chicago River, is one of the ugliest things that malicious human perversity ever produced in the name of social welfare—the notorious Cabrini Green housing project.

Certainly no one did St. Frances Xavier Cabrini a favor by naming that place after her. In Cabrini Green there really is social disorganization, created not so much by the black people who live there as by the insane urban renewal, public housing, and welfare policies which professional do-gooders, liberals, and reformers (many of them heavily influenced by the concepts of the Chicago School) established to "help" the blacks. The housing that Cabrini Green replaced was for the most part unredeemable slum. For all its ugliness, physically Cabrini Green may be an improvement; the plumbing works most of the time, and the death rates there are far lower than in the Stanislowowo across the river a half century ago; but humanly, Cabrini Green is much worse. There was hope, there was expectation, there was some kind of self-confidence in the Stanislowowo. There is none of these things in Cabrini Green. And it is not because there are fundamental cultural differences between blacks and Poles but because the Poles were spared ministrations of social welfare policymakers who set out to help. The Poles were lucky; the professional do-gooders never did like them. The blacks were unlucky to be the victims of their help.

There ought to be ways to help the poor without making them dependent. There ought to be ways to renew neighborhoods without destroying them. There ought to be ways to replace old housing stock without putting up ready-made slums that generate destructive crime and violence which radiate far beyond their boundaries. There ought to be, but the bureaucrats, administrators, and the planners, the sociology professors, and the wise men who dream great dreams about urban life don't seem to be able to come up with any such schemes. It would never occur to them to look for answers by turning to places like Bridgeport and the Stanislowowo.

We go north a few blocks from Cabrini Green and come to Old Town—still just a stone's throw across the river from the Stanislowowo. It is not the honky tonk Old Town of Wells Street but the Old Town north of North Avenue on such streets as Sedgewick and Larrabee. "Lincoln Park" the students of the Chicago School would call it. When my father lived on Sedgewick Street, he and his family didn't know that it was "Old Town" or "Lincoln Park," they just knew that it was Sedgewick Street. And my father, who had a fine sense of Celtic irony, would have been fascinated by what happened to his block. I walk down the street, trusty camera in hand, and come upon the house which I think was the one in which my father lived. I could probably buy that house today for something in excess of $150,000.

Two or three blocks in one direction and you have the horror of Cabrini Green, two or three blocks in the other direction and you get vacant land (urban renewal), and in another block or two the most ugly desolation of an abandoned neighborhood; but here you have a sophisticated new urban professional class, remodeling and rehabilitating old homes to become smart, fashionable town houses whose interiors and exteriors are frequently the subject of feature articles in newspapers and magazines. Some of the lakefront liberals have come down from their high rises and moved out toward Halsted Street, and further north, at a somewhat safer remove from Cabrini Green, one hears tales of whole blocks of Latinos being dispossessed by developers who are rehabilitating the old houses in preparation for the advent of yet more young professionals. That's the trouble; you let one young professional on your block and pretty soon the whole block goes. Besides they all look alike and think alike. Would you want your sister to marry one?

Within a three-mile radius of the center of the city of Chicago, in other words, most of the old slums have been removed, leaving a very considerable number of quaint, attractive old homes on lovely tree-lined streets, which with a little better lighting and improved plumbing and several coats of paint become highly attractive and desirable places in which to live. So great is the chaos and anarchy which passes for city planning that it is often a matter of chance whether a given street is abandoned, destroyed by the wrecking ball, turned into a high-rise public housing monstrosity, left vacant like Berlin after the blitz, rehabilitated for the suburban professional class, or kept a multilingual, multiracial, multiethnic community. (In the case of Bridgeport, of course, it is also a matter of political clout.) You tell yourself there has to be a better way.

Four Streets

Bridgeport . . . Maxwell Street . . . Taylor Street . . .
Noble Avenue . . . Washington Boulevard . . . Little Italy
. . . Little Hell . . . the places we tried to leave behind
. . . only some of them managed to survive . . .
quite well, thank you. . . .

At various times in the last seventy-five years Chicago has been either the largest or the second largest Polish, Lithuanian, Jewish, Swedish, and Irish city in the world. If the United States is a nation of immigrants, Chicago is the city of immigrants. It was created after 1850, and there is not now and never has been the native elite of the sort one could find in New York, Boston, and Philadelphia—not even pale imitations of the Cabots, the Lodges, the Biddles, and the Drexels.

But because we are the offspring of immigrants and because we are still so close to their experience, it is frequently hard for us to grasp the size of the immigration phenomenon in the city on the southern shores of Lake Michigan.

The statistics are staggering. Between 1850, when the "Famine Irish" and the "Revolution Germans" began to arrive, and 1914, when the First World War turned off the immigration flow, more than 800,000 foreigners came to Chicago—almost 300,000 in the first decade and a half of this century alone. In 1910, 77 per cent of the city were either immigrants or children of immigrants. Bohemians, Irish, Germans, and Swedes came mostly before 1900. After the turn of the century, the tidal waves of Poles, Italians, and eastern European Jews reached their height. In some years Chicago must have received more than 50,000 immigrants, almost all of them poor, uneducated, land-hungry peasants.

In 1886, there were 45,000 Poles in Chicago; in 1900, there were 150,000. By the time the restrictive (anti-Slavic, anti-Italian) immigration laws were passed in 1920, there were 400,000 Poles in the city. When the First World War began there were 75,000 Lithuanians in Chicago, a surge of 73,000 in less than twenty years. In 1890, there were only a relative handful of Italians in the city—13,000. The number doubled to 26,000 by the turn of the century—still a relatively small figure. But by 1920, there were more than 124,000 Italians in Chicago.

These statistics alone may make us gasp, but the proportions of the phenomenon become astonishing when we try to picture in our imaginations what it was like.

Four streets tell the story of a city that was.

MAXWELL STREET

The street is almost empty on the cold, gray day of early winter. Many of the stands are folded, almost all the others are closed. A few frigid merchants haggle with dark-skinned customers. Halsted, the big street which crosses Maxwell, is still a street of small shops and crowded windows. An occasional battered old frame house or abandoned brick two-flat can be seen off in the background; but all that remains of the Jewish ghetto is the open street market of Maxwell Street and some empty lots. You close your eyes, though, and the sights and the sounds, and the smells come back—kosher butcher shops filled with sausages, basement fish stores (where you could buy ready-made gefilte fish), the bearded horseradish grinder, the bake shops with poppy seed bread and bagels, the bath house (with a special section for the women's *mikveh*), the tiny theater, the second-story book stores, the cafes filled with arguing intellectuals, the cigar stores, the gambling houses (where organized crime of a sort was already going strong), the lawyers, the wine dealers, the ward heelers, the petty politicians, the "real-estateniks," the small synagogues with their impoverished rabbinical scholars, the old women in wigs, the old men with beards, the noise of the "pullers" selling their wares, the dust swirling in the hot breeze of summer, the pervasive smell of garlic.

It's all gone now. The dark-skinned people there are not Jews but Latinos. Soon there will be no one alive who remembers the old ghetto —or even the newer one further west on Douglas Boulevard. The children and grandchildren have moved to Skokie and have created a new kind of "ghetto without walls," a prosperous place where the Ph.D. replaces the talmudic scholar.

Maxwell Street afforded a hard living a half century ago, and maybe it is best forgotten. You are glad the third and fourth generations have fuller, richer, and more open lives where they are now. Yet the energy, the vitality, the ambition of the ghetto survived; you have to admire the people who lived there and honor them in the memory of their first place.

ROOSEVELT ROAD—HOLY FAMILY PARISH

A few blocks north of Maxwell Street on Roosevelt Road the land has returned to the prairies—not the prairie of virgin land but that of urban renewal. The great gray facade of Holy Family Church seems to be eroding; next door, St. Ignatius College huddles close to the church, conscious, perhaps, that its days are numbered. Behind the church there is a school yard filled with black and Latino young people, and the buildings by it are painted in bright "street-mural modern." Some of the old wooden houses have been modernized, and the brick homes are vivid in their new paint jobs. The "back end" of Holy Family parish is being "rehabbed"; the young professionals from the university and the medical center are beginning to move in. The neighborhood may once again be the magnet that it was in the 1860s when the Irish began to swarm into the "church of the prairies."

It is not hard to imagine how the new Holy Family must have looked —the largest church in North America then—in Arnold Damen's time. The Jesuit knew the Irish were coming and would settle wherever the church was. And now the prairies stretch out toward downtown Chicago just as they did then, but it is the downtown of the Sears Tower, not of the ramshackle buildings of the Civil War era.

The Irish came—canal workers, common laborers, policemen, priests, politicians; and they were loud, argumentative, hard drinking. They rallied around their church and their schools, desperately striving for respectability in a country which did not want them. They were willing to give up anything except their religion to achieve acceptance. Poetry, mysticism, the lovely Gaelic language—all would go. And with the memory of the Great Famine still fresh, they heeded the urgings of their priests to become full-fledged Americans. They would be Americans even if they had to leave virtually everything behind. So they worked and died in the sewers and the ditches, their women pushed accounting machines at Sears for five dollars a week, they clawed and pushed and struggled to get through first high school and then college. They took over the city government and robbed it in retribution for the life's blood that was extracted from them by the city and its people. And when the Chicago Fire swept through the wooden tinderbox streets to the very boundaries of their parish, they rallied to the church building and characteristically took full credit when the wind changed and the neighborhood was saved.

The Irish are gone now—though the church they left behind is full of their ghosts. For you it is the most haunted church in America, because you still see your own ancestors doggedly slogging through the mud to church on a cold, wet November Sunday. No matter how bad the weather, how sick the head of the house was at home, how overworked and tired his spouse, they maintained that one link with their past and their God.

In the comfortable professional-class homes in Oak Park, River Forest, and Park Ridge, do the Irish remember the people whose ghosts walk at Holy Family? For a long time they tried to forget them, but the memories are crowding back.

LEXINGTON AND TAYLOR STREETS—VERNON PARK

Vernon Park still stands gallant and defiant. Neither an expressway nor a great, cold university campus could wipe it out completely. The new construction going on just off Taylor Street makes you think that the neighborhood may have the last laugh on the university which almost destroyed it. At one end of the park is Mother Cabrini Hospital (once Columbus Hospital). Poor Mother Cabrini—they did two terrible things to her, they made her a saint and they named an ugly, evil housing project after her. She deserved better. How many doctors and lawyers, architects and city planners, priests and "outfit" leaders survived the first minutes and hours of life because of the hospital she built with little more than sheer will power?

On the Lexington Street side of the park there are elegant row houses that remind you for a moment of London. The great dome of the "French church" looms behind them and Our Lady of Pompeii is tucked into a corner of the park. You remember that this end of the old neighborhood was where the Italian middle class lived. The poor stayed on the other side of Morgan, and there were poor aplenty in the old neighborhood—many of them kept in the semislavery of the *padrone* system by their own countrymen. Most of the earliest arrivals couldn't read or write and were easily exploited; but they gave all they had (which was mostly hard work) and eked their way ahead to "middle-class" jobs, many of which were political—street sweepers, sewer diggers, asphalt helpers, road graders, garbage collectors, and streetcar company employees. A few, a relatively few, turned to gambling and later, with the coming of that noble experiment in national virtue called Prohibition, to bootlegging—which made you lots of money but ensured a short life to enjoy it.

The Italians lacked the urban skills of their Jewish neighbors and the language advantage of the Irish. They were kept in political bondage by the notorious Irish politicians, the worst among them being Johnny Powers ("Johnny de Pow"), the prince of boodlers, and they were harassed by the pushy do-gooders from Hull House. Still, they too have made the American dream come true, and if many of them remain in Vernon Park, sharing it with the more recent immigrants (many of whom live in the low-rise housing project on the south side of the park), the reason is not that they are too poor to leave; rather they don't want to leave, and the peculiar accidents of urban development have left part of their neighborhood to them.

And heaven help anyone who tries to take it away from them now.

NOBLE STREET—THE "POLISH CORRIDOR"

Noble from Division Street to Chicago Avenue is quiet and uncrowded. Now the "Noble Square" mall cuts off the corridor in mid-passage. The homes there are neat and brightly painted, and although most of the faces are black and Latino, there are still unmistakably Slavic children tripping happily home from school. You are in the heart of the "Stanislowowo" or "Polish downtown." Chicago is the second largest Polish city in the world, and "St. Stan's" of fifty years ago was the largest parish in the United States with its 40,000 members. Just down the block is its offspring and archrival, Holy Trinity. When feelings ran strong between the "nationals" of the Trojcowo and the "clericals" of the Stanislowowo, the parishioners from these two strongholds would battle one another in the streets, and the Chicago police—doubtless baffled by the cause—had to be called in to restore order. Both groups were intensely loyal Americans, fiercely devout Catholics and passionately patriotic Poles, but they had, to say the least, strong differences of opinion as to how those three elements should be combined. Still, when Wincenty Barzynski, the giant of the Stanislowowo, died, his rival pastor, Casimir Sztuczko walked down Noble Street to join the mourning for one of the greatest immigrant leaders the country would ever know. And it was down that same street several years later that both groups joined hands in celebration of the election of the first Polish-American bishop, Paul Rhode, and the return of peace to Noble Street.

These were the poorest of the poor; they had little else in life besides their religion. In the first two decades of this century, the population density of the ten square blocks around the old church on Pulaski Park was three times higher than Tokyo's or Calcutta's. The air was foul, the plumbing inadequate or nonexistent, and even mild rain showers filled the basement apartments with raw sewage, frequently up to knee level. There were more than two hundred uncovered manure boxes in the area, and the death rate was more than thirty-seven per thousand.

A typical Pole was making less than eight dollars per week, paying more than that a month for his three-room apartment. Nor was there any Prentice Marshall to enforce job quotas. The Poles had the worst jobs in the city and got the worst pay. The city's elites considered them and the Italians racially inferior; the Italians were inherently criminal, the Poles naturally tense and high strung with a woefully deteriorated family life. Was it not true that half the juvenile gangs in Chicago were Polish?

And in those days no one screamed "racism!" against such "common wisdom."

Many of the more recent immigrants on Noble Street are poor too —poorer than anyone should be in American society, but the backyard houses, the basement toilets, the manure heaps, the sweatshops above the barns, and the miniscule apartments are gone. So, too, are most of the Poles who made it out of poverty into the middle and upper middle classes. Noble Street stands as their monument and a still vital memory.

There are other streets—South Halsted with its Greek restaurants, Archer Road, where America's greatest philosopher, the incomparable Martin Dooley, held forth. There is also 18th Street where the Latins have replaced the Bohemians and the multisteepled streets of Bridge-port. On such streets the Chicago that is came to be.

As the memories come alive again, one is struck by how young the people on Maxwell, Taylor, Noble, and Roosevelt streets were. Many of them came unmarried or just married. We think of the immigrants as old because we remember the immigrant grandparent tucked away in the back bedroom. It is startling to realize them in the strength, the vigor, and courage of youth—most of them unskilled, many of them illiterate, virtually all of them possessing nothing other than a dream and ambition. They were the land-hungry peasants driven by popula-tion expansion, tyranny, and revolution from a Europe which invited desertion. America did them no favors. The German sociologist Max Weber wrote home to his doting wife about Chicago: "The Greek shining the Yankee's shoes for five cents, the German acting as his waiter, the Irish managing his politics, and the Italian digging his dirty ditches." He didn't even notice the Poles cleaning up the mess in the stockyards.

No, America did not like them and did not want them. It quickly threw up a barrier against more of them coming, and it oppressed and exploited those who had arrived already. But it left them free to work, to save, to own—and that was more than they had in the world they left behind. So work and save they did, and eventually they owned, and then, despite the confident predictions of all their betters, they climbed up out of the slum, went to college, became professionals, and made their impossible dream come true—for which few of them get credit from a society which replaced the legal restrictions the Dillingham Commission recommended with the new stereotypes of the ethnic joke and restrictive hiring and promotion practices in elite-dominated fields (the media and foundation worlds, for example).

A few of the immigrants achieved their dream in their own time; others lived to see and to enjoy the success of their children and grandchildren; still others died wondering whether the dream would ever replace the nightmare reality in which they had lived. From what one knows of them, they did not doubt too much; they hoped and even expected the fruition of their dream. After all, they were Americans.

What did these immigrants give to the city? Everything. They gave all they had and built all that is Chicago. They and their children and grandchildren are Chicago—the overwhelming majority of its people and its productive workers. They were the carpenters, the plumbers, the steam fitters, the steel workers, the doctors, the lawyers, the street cleaners, the precinct captains, the solderers, the school teachers, the cops, the clergy, the liquor store owners, the undertakers, the grocers, the city planners, and now—though they are not welcome everywhere —the scholars, the artists, and the novelists. They gave to the city their hopes, their dreams, their hard work, their energy, their ambition. The Lakeshore-Hyde Park aristocracy may look down their noses at the descendants of the immigrants and ignore them completely, or worse, patronize them. Without the immigrants, Chicago would not be.

But in the upper-middle-class fringe sections and suburbs, the Irish, the Poles, the Italians, the Greeks, the Jews, the Bohemians are not themselves always easy about the immigrant past that is still so close to them. One may be proud of one's ancestors but yet a little embarrassed by them. They often seem to have been crude and not altogether "respectable." One may appreciate their sacrifices but still not thank them for them. The romance, the adventure, the tragedy of their lives are still things one does not like to think about too often. They did too much for us. Indeed, who and what would we be were it not for them?

Our ambivalence is not surprising. One does not like to have to remember the poverty of the 1910s, the fierce nativism of the 1920s, the grim frustration of the Great Depression. Some things are too painful and powerful in memory yet to dwell upon. It all takes time.

Yet there will come a time between the second and third centennials when Americans—all Americans—will come to admire and respect the urban pioneers, those brave young men and women who came to Chicago seeking what the Poles called *nowy swiat*—a "new world," a new life. With their lives they bought our lives. We will be in their debt forever.

The Ethnic Miracle

No matter what street you live on
you can find ethnic restaurants nearby . . .
Greek . . . German . . . Sicilian . . . Chinese . . .
Polish . . . and of course the Irish tavern . . .
even the neighborhood candy store has survived . . .
sometimes, as Liam will tell you, better than ever.

This neighborhood is a ten-square-block area with almost 14,000 people, an average of 39.8 inhabitants per acre—three times that of the most crowded portions of Tokyo, Calcutta, and many other Asian cities. One block contains 1,349 children; a third of the neighborhood's 771 buildings are built on "back lots" behind existing structures. The buildings are divided into 2,796 apartments, with an average of 3.7 rooms per apartment. More than three-quarters of the apartments have less than 400 square feet, 556 of them are in basements which quickly become awash with human excrement during even mild rainstorms. Garbage disposal is a chronic problem—usually it is simply dumped in the narrow passageways between buildings. The death rate is 37.2 per thousand. Desertion, juvenile delinquency, mental disorders, and prostitution have the highest rates in the city. Social disorganization in this neighborhood, according to all outside observers—even the sympathetic ones—is practically total and irredeemable.

Blacks? Latinos? Inhabitants of some Third World city? No. Poles in Chicago in 1920.

The neighborhood is still there. You drive in from O'Hare Airport and see the towering spires of St. Mary of the Angels, St. Stanislaus Kostka, Holy Trinity. If you turn off at Division Street you will see that the manure boxes are gone, and so are the backyard buildings, the outdoor plumbing, the sweatshops over the barns, the tuberculosis, the family disorganization, the violence, and the excessive death rates.

The Poles are gone too for the most part, having moved further northwest along Milwaukee Avenue and out into the suburbs—a prosperous middle class. How have they managed to make it, this most despised of all the white immigrant groups? It is no exaggeration to say that no one really knows. The success of the southern and eastern European immigrant groups who frantically crowded into the United States before the First World War is as unexplained as it is astonishing.

Yet the "ethnic miracle" is one of the most fascinating stories in the history of the United States, an American success story, an accomplishment of the "system" in spite of itself; and while it does not necessarily provide a paradigm for imitation by later groups (in fact, it almost certainly does not), the ethnic miracle does offer insights into how American society works that social policymakers can ill afford to ignore.

The neighborhood described above is the Stanislowowo, that area in Chicago filled with the "Polish cathedrals" we saw in Chapter 2, and which is bisected by Noble Street, the "Polish corridor" of Chapter 3. Its ignorant, illiterate, dirty, diseased inhabitants in the years between 1900 and 1920 spoke little English if any at all; their families, the sociologists at the time assured us, were chronically "disorganized." They had no tradition of freedom and responsibility; they lacked political maturity. They were a bad bet to assimilate into American society.

Was there poverty and suffering in the Stanislowowo and the neighborhoods like it? That was largely the fault of the immigrants themselves, Americans were assured by their elites, and the walls of restrictive legislation to end immigration were thrown up after the end of the war. Large-scale Americanization campaigns were begun to try to teach these illiterate peasants the virtues of good Americans, and great hope was placed in the public high school as the institution which would mold the children of the immigrants (the parents were clearly impossible) into good, loyal, dutiful Americans.

There were no quotas, no affirmative action, no elaborate system of social services, and, heaven knows, no ethnic militancy to force reforms. (It does not follow, incidentally, that there should not be these things for the more recent immigrants to the big cities of the United States.) There was no talk of reparation, no sense of guilt, no feelings of compassion for these immigrants. The stupid, brutal but pathetic heros of Nelson Algren's novels were about as far as most Americans got; and *Scarface* and *Little Caesar* of the motion pictures were taken to be typical of the Italians who got beyond street cleaning, ditch digging, garbage collection, and waiting on tables. It is safe to say that in the twentieth century, no urban immigrants have been so systematically hated and despised by the nation's cultural and intellectual elites. The stereotypes may be more sophisticated now, but they still portray the southern and eastern European ethnics as hateful and despicable. Stanley Kowalski has been replaced by Don Corleone, but both still represent the white ethnic. And the popular image of the collective white ethnic remains that of the blue-collar, racist, hard-hat, chauvinist hawk even though available statistical evidence supports neither the Godfather nor the bigot myth and lends no credence to the ethnic joke.

Closely related to the thesis of the racial inferiority of the eastern and southern European immigrants was the theory of their cultural inferiority.

"Social disorganization" was the explanation of the plight of the Stanislowowians adduced by the Chicago School of sociology. The cultural values of the immigrants were not able to absorb the shock of the immigration experience and the resultant confrontation with the more "modern" values of the host society. Crime, generational conflict, family disorganization, prostitution and juvenile delinquency were the effects of this unequal meeting of a modern and a peasant culture. Several generations of scholars, administrators and social workers were raised on *The Gang, Gold Coast and the Slum*, and *The Polish Peasant in Europe and America*—which were in whole or in part about the Stanislowowo; and much of the reform legislation of the thirties was designed out of a social disorganization perspective. The problem with the poor was not their poverty but their social disorganization and "alienation." Fortunately for the ethnics they stopped being poor before the reformers could set up high-rise public housing and dependency-producing welfare legislation to "undisorganize" them.

Across the Chicago River from "St. Stan's" is the infamous Cabrini Green high-rise public housing project, one of the most evil things that human good intentions has ever produced—a monstrosity which causes the very social disorganization which it was designed to eliminate. It is a slum far worse than the author of *The Gold Coast and the Slum* could have imagined; and while the death rate may not be as high as it was in the Stanislowowo in 1901, the human demoralization in Cabrini Green is far worse. (Cooley High of movie fame was once the parochial high school for St. Stan's.) If present welfare, urban renewal, and public housing legislation had existed a half century ago, the Poles might still be poor; and sociologists might still be writing books about how the Polish family structure—one of the strongest in America—is "disorganized."

One does not therefore conclude that there ought to be no government intervention to help and protect the poor. On the contrary, the ethnic miracle might have happened more quickly if the government had intervened to prevent discrimination against them and to facilitate their rise out of poverty. But the "ethnic miracle" at least raises questions as to whether social legislation would not be much more effective if it respects the culture and family life of the poor and fights poverty directly rather than with mostly useless attempts to correct "alienation" and "social disorganization." Obviously there are individuals and families which have been so badly traumatized either by poverty or by misguided efforts to "unalienate" them (or combinations of both) that they cannot cope with problems of urban living without help from society. But the "ethnic miracle" suggests that such help ought not be geared to make them think and act like psychiatrically oriented social workers but rather like the more successful members of their own cultural community.

A half century ago the "disorganization" models of the Chicago School looked like a big change from the biological racism of the Immigration Commission. In retrospect, and in light of the "ethnic miracle," one is permitted to wonder if in fact the theory of social disorganization was not a more subtle but equally pernicious form of cultural racism—and one not by any means absent from the reform legislation of the 1960s.

The twenties and thirties were bad times for the immigrants and their children. The fierce nativism of the twenties, the grim and frustrating Great Depression of the thirties kept them pretty much in the poverty of the immigrant neighborhoods. Only a few managed to claw their way out into middle-class respectability. But in the three decades since the end of the Second World War, an extraordinary economic and social phenomenon has occurred: the ethnics have made it. The Italians are now the third richest religio-ethnic group in American society—second only to Jews and Irish Catholics—and the Poles earn almost $1,000 a year more than the average white American in metropolitan areas of the North. In the middle 1940s, the curve of college attendance for young people for both Italians and Poles began to swing upward, so that by the 1960s, Poles and Italians of college age were *more* likely to attend college than the national average for white Americans.

Without anyone's noticing it, those who were doomed by their race, their religion, their language, and their family backgrounds to be failures have succeeded. Few of them are wealthy, some are still poor; but on the average their incomes are substantially higher than those of other white Americans living in the same cities and regions of the United States. Many Americans reject in principle the possibility of such a miracle, and some of the ethnic leaders themselves (in a perhaps unintentional ethnic joke) vigorously deny the success of their own people; yet the data are beyond any reasonable doubt: in a very short space of time, the length of one generation, more or less, the American dream has come true; and some of the people who were children in the Stanislowowo in 1920 have lived to see and to enjoy the achievement of their dream.

Even the Stanislowowo has changed for those who remain. The well-fed, neatly dressed, scrupulously clean children who troop out of St. Stanislaus Kostka on a spring afternoon—grandchildren, perhaps, of the women who worked in sweatshops filled with the stench of manure sixty hours a week—are clearly the offspring of an affluent society.

There is doubtless much wrong with the United States of America, but sometimes things have gone well—almost despite conscious efforts to make them go badly. The success of the eastern and southern European immigrant groups of the turn of the century is one of the United States' success stories. The achievements of the Jews have been well known for some time; only recently have we discovered that the Italians and the Poles have also done remarkably well. We do not like to admit it. Very few agencies or scholars, whose responsibility it is to study and understand American society, show any interest at all in the extraordinary success story of those against whom the immigration acts of 1920 were directed. It seems that we couldn't care less about finding an explanation.

Perhaps it was the public school; maybe education was the answer, and good, solid American education undid the work of a thousand years of oppression and misery. The evidence, however, suggests the opposite. The Polish and Italian success seems to have come first in income, then in education, and finally in occupation (and, as we shall see later, they are still impeded somewhat in occupational achievement).*

The few scholars who pay any attention to immigration have begun to wonder whether the education-occupation-income progression toward economic success is all that helpful a paradigm. Among the Asian immigrants to the United States and the Sephardic Jews in Israel income parity seems to come before educational and occupational parity. In the Sephardic families, for example, with everyone working —husband, wife, and children—equality of family income with the

---

*The empirical evidence on which these conclusions are based comes from an analysis of a composite file put together from twelve National Opinion Research Center (NORC) national sample surveys. (A complete report will be published under the title *Ethnicity, Denomination and Inequality* by Sage Publications, Beverly Hills, California.) The composite sample numbers some 18,000 respondents, and, despite serious limitations, still represents the best collection of data currently available on American religio-ethnic groups. The U.S. Census cannot ask a religious question, and only recently has the Census' monthly Current Population Survey begun to ask one intermittently. However, since Polish Jews and Polish Catholics are combined under the rubric "Pole," and Irish Protestants (disproportionately rural southerners and more numerous than Catholics) are combined with Irish Catholics, the Current Population Survey data are of utility only for Italians. The NORC composite statistics, however, have been compared with the results of the Current Population Survey (50,000 respondents). There are only slight variations between the two; in the case of the Italians, a group for which the NORC data and CPS data are roughly comparable, there is virtually no difference in the statistics on education, occupation, and income. Unfortunately until funding agencies are willing to support better data collection, composite survey data will provide the only available evidence for scholarly investigation.

All comparisons in this article are with white, non-Latin Americans living within standard metropolitan statistical areas outside of the South. These are the areas of the country where the overwhelming majority of the ethnics are concentrated and where income, occupation, and education tend to be higher than in nonmetropolitan northern and southern locations.

Ashkenazy has already been achieved, although educational and occupational parity lags behind. It would seem very likely that most immigrant groups must first achieve some kind of basic financial success, and only then can they exploit the advantages of educational and occupational mobility and concomittant opportunities for even more dramatic income achievement.

However patriarchal the family structures may have been, the womenfolk of the ethnic immigrants went to work from the beginning —long before it became an upper-middle-class fashion. Doubtless the income of many wage earners in a family provided an economic base for the ethnics to make their initial breakthrough, which occurred, perhaps, sometime in the early 1950s. (Data on neighborhood concentration of various ethnic communities indicate that the Poles finally began to move out from the center of the city in proper proportion at that time.) But by 1970, the women in Polish and Italian families were no more likely to have jobs than their nonethnic counterparts in the large cities of the North. So the income achievement of the southern and eastern European Catholics cannot be explained by multiple wage earners in the family—though there is a possibility that many of the men and some of the women may also have second and third jobs.*

The income achievement of Poles and Italians is all the more remarkable when one considers that their occupational and educational achievement still lags slightly behind that of other white Americans living in big cities of the North. (Though their educational *mobility*— the increase in educational level above that of one's parents—is the highest in the country.) Thus in metropolitan regions of the North in 1974, Italian family income was $1,254 above the average and Polish

*Nor does the twenty-five years of prosperity between 1945 and 1970 explain the ethnic miracle, though it obviously created an environment in which a miracle could occur. For not only did the ethnics improve their income during that quarter century, as did virtually everyone else, but they improved it disproportionately. At the end of the quarter century, they were not only better off than they were in 1945, they had improved their relative position in comparison with the rest of the population. Prosperity, in other words, provided the opportunity for the ethnic miracle, but the miracle itself was a response to the opportunity.

income, $813. However, when one compared the Italians and the Poles with other northern urbanites with the same educational and occupational backgrounds, the net advantage of the ethnics went up substantially—Italians to $3,684, the Poles to $1,427. Poles and Italians, in other words, *do* more with their education and occupation than do other Americans.

A word should be said in passing about a slightly earlier ethnic miracle, that of the Irish Catholics, who are the richest, best-educated, and the most occupationally prestigious of any gentile group in the land —the comparison again being made with their appropriate counterparts, those living in metropolitan regions in the North. Irish Catholic college attendance for those of college age surpassed the national average as long ago as 1910, and has remained substantially above the average ever since, passing even the Episcopalians in the 1960s. The Irish Catholic income advantage over other northern metropolitans is over $2,000 a year (trailing behind the $3,000 a year of Jews). Many of those who are willing to admit that the Poles and the Italians may have achieved rough parity with the rest of the country find the spectacular success of Irish Catholics almost impossible to swallow.

There may be an important social policy hint in the apparent primacy of income in the "assimilation" of the early twentieth-century immigrants. Subject to much more careful investigation, one might want to take it as a tentative hypothesis that the school is a rather poor institution at facilitating the upward mobility of minority groups— *until* such groups first acquire some kind of routh income parity. The naive American faith that equality of education produces equality of income seems to have been stood on its head in the case of the ethnics. For them, better income meant more effective education.*

---

*It should be noted that I do not intend to suggest a comparison between the white immigrants of the turn of the century and the more recent nonwhite immigrants to the city. The path of upward mobility which worked for one group at one time does not necessarily work for another group at another time. Comparisons may be interesting and suggestive, but they ought not to be pushed too far. The Polish immigrants were indeed abject and miserable, unwanted and humiliated; but they were still white. On the other hand, the apparent historical phenomenon of income preceding rather

Nor did the public schools play the critical "Americanization" role that such educators as Dr. James B. Conant expected them to play in the 1940s and 1950s. Even taking into account parents' education and income, the most successful educationally, occupationally, and economically of the ethnics went to parochial schools—and they did so at a time when the schools were even more overcrowded than they are today, staffed by even less adequately trained teachers, and administered by an even smaller educational bureaucracy than the very small one which somehow or other manages to keep the parochial schools going today. Again, a social policy hint: maybe what counts about schools for a minority group is, as my colleague Professor William McCready has remarked, "They are *our* schools" (whoever "we" may be).

So one must still face the puzzle: despite the virtually unanimous opinion of educated Americans a half century ago, the children and the grandchildren of eastern and southern European immigrants have achieved not only economic equality but economic superiority, on the average, in the United States. They were not supposed to be able to do it; to many people it is incredible that they have done it; and to almost everyone the explanation of their success is obscure. Now we see that the ethnics in the quarter century between the end of the Second World War and the end of the Vietnam War did exactly what the Jews had done in the previous quarter century—and they did it with apparent ease.

---

than following education for the ethnics does seem to add weight to the argument of those who presently are wondering whether too much has been expected of education as a corrective of social pathology in the last two decades. The experience of the ethnics is interesting in itself; whatever hints for current social policy may be obtained from their study ought to be considered no more than that—certainly not as blueprints for imitation. Occasionally one hears an ethnic complain, "Why can't 'they' work hard like we did?" but the evidence shows that most ethnics are well aware that nonwhites have to put up with greater obstacles. The irony of their comment is aimed not so much at the more recent immigrants but rather at those of the intellectual and cultural elite who despised the ethnics when they were poor and have contempt for them now that they are middle class. As the Irishman said, "Where were youse when we needed help?"

How come?

The immigrants themselves were ambitious. Perhaps they were the enterprising and courageous young people in their own societies —and young they were. When we see movies like *Hester Street*, many of us are astonished to discover that the immigrants from eastern and southern Europe were disproportionately young and either unmarried or just married. We all have a recollection of an old grandparent whom we knew during childhood, and without giving the matter much thought, we tend to imagine the immigrants themselves as old—forgetting that the old *babushka* or *mamacita* was once as young as we were.

The immigrants came from a Europe which, as one American historian has remarked, "invited desertion." The population expansion of the middle nineteenth century had created a land-hungry peasant class for whom there was no room either on the farms or in the cities. They came to the United States seeking "the good life," the kind of life that owning land made possible. They were fully prepared to work hard; indeed, a life of anything but hard work was beyond their comprehension. They would work hard to make money. "All the Italians want is money," remarked an observer during the 1910s, and like devout practitioners of the Protestant ethic, they would sacrifice to save as much money as they could. In 1905, when Poles were still pouring into the city of Chicago, 15 per cent of the money in Chicago savings and loan institutions was already in Polish-owned associations, a remarkable achievement for people who were scarcely off the boat. Credit buying was taboo. "Cash money" paid for everything. Desperately poor people themselves, with scores of generations of poverty behind them, the immigrants could imagine no other way to live besides scrimping, sacrificing, saving. America did them no favors, gave them no special treatment; in fact discriminated against them, forced them into the most menial occupations, the most miserable housing, and exploited them through the most corrupt political structures in the country. Americans hated them, despised them, condemned them, and eventually tried to bar their relatives from joining them; they joked about them, stereotyped them, tried to change them into "good Americans" by making them ashamed of their own heritages.

The Poles and the Italians, like the Irish and the Jews before them, bitterly resented such treatment; but they did not grow angry at the United States, for even though it did them no favors, it still provided them with two things they would never had had in the old country: personal freedom and the opportunity to convert the hard work they took for granted into economic progress. In the old country, hard work got you nothing; in the United States it got you, or at least your children or their children, a chance.

Hard work, saving, sacrifice—such is a tentative explanation of the ethnic miracle. Ironically, the Catholic ethnics turned out to be very good at these "Protestant" and "American" traits which the Dillingham Commission thought they could never learn. To work hard, to save, to be ambitious for oneself and one's children: the immigrants needed no "Americanization" to learn that way of life. They came here with a dream; it was not that they expected something for nothing but rather that their hard work would earn them something. For some of them, for many of their children, and for most of their grandchildren the dream came true.

Is that how it happened?

It would seem so, though until much more careful study of the history of immigrant families is done, we will not know for sure. And it should be done in the relatively near future while some of the immigrants and their oldest children are still alive to be interviewed. But curiously enough, many Americans, including ethnics like Michael Novak, are much more eager to believe that the American dream has not come true for the ethnics. If it hasn't, there is nothing then to explain.

In the process of economic achievement, have the ethnics "assimilated"? Have they absorbed the values and beliefs and behavior patterns of the host culture? To begin with, they came with many values in common. They were, after all, products of the same white European, Judeo-Christian heritage. They learned to speak English quickly, to wear the same clothes, listen to the same radio and television programs, read the same newspapers; and yet a remarkable diversity of values, attitudes, styles, opinions, and behavior has persisted. Affection and authority, for example, are recognizably different in the Jewish, the Italian, the Polish, and the Irish families, as are the styles with which each approaches politics, the ways in which each consumes alcohol, and the ultimate views each holds about the nature of human nature and the nature of the universe.

Furthermore, these differences do not seem to diminish with the number of generations one has been in the United States or with the amount of education one has had. In a loose pluralistic society like the United States, you can achieve economic success and rather harmonious adjustment to other groups while still maintaining a partially distinctive culture of your own. Indeed, you can maintain such a distinctive culture without having to be self-conscious about it. The Irish propensity for politics and alcohol, for example, and the Polish propensity to vote (Poles have the highest voting rates of any American religio-ethnic group) are not affected by whether one is self-conscious or militant about one's Irishness or Polishness. The anxiety of the Dillingham Commission and its nativist successors about whether diversity threatened America's "common culture" missed the whole point: in America the common culture validates diversity. You can be anything you want religiously, culturally, stylistically so long as you are committed to the fundamental political principles of the republic.

Ethnicity is not a way of looking back to the old world. Most of the immigrants were only too happy to get the hell out of it. Ethnicity is rather a way of being American, a way of defining yourself into the pluralistic culture which existed before you arrived. The last thing in the world the new ethnic upper middle class wants is to define themselves out of the common American culture. Why should they? America may have done them no favors, but it still has been better to them than any society their families ever knew.

So the militant ethnic somewhere out there in "middle America," hard hat on his head and gun in his hand ready to tear the larger society apart in resisting the advances of the nonwhite immigrants, is almost entirely a fiction of the imagination of the liberal left in the media and the academy. The ethnic may not always like some of the things he sees and hears on television, but his standard of living has at least doubled in the last quarter century so he is not angry at the American way; he is not about to do anything to endanger his still precarious respectability and affluence. He may rejoice that the black activism of the 1960s has legitimated his somewhat more explicit and conscious pride in heritage, but the "ethnic revival" or the "new ethnic militancy" is largely another fiction of the liberal imagination.

Nor has the ethnic turned to the right. He is neither a "rugged individualist" nor a political reactionary, as many left liberal commentators would so dearly like to believe. On social legislation, the Italian, Polish, and, for that matter, Irish Catholics are still left of center, still members of the New Deal coalition. They did not disproportionately defect from the Democratic Party to vote against George McGovern, nor were they strong supporters of George Wallace in the 1968 presidential election. The myth of the massive Polish vote for Wallace is so powerful that it is practically impossible to debunk; yet the Poles were the most likely of all gentile groups to vote for Hubert Humphrey, and substantially less than the 6 per cent nonsouthern vote for Wallace was recorded among Polish Catholics. It would surely be inaccurate to think of the children, grandchildren and great grandchildren of the ethnics as left-wing liberals or militant integrationists (most militants seem to live in the suburbs), but on virtually every political and social issue facing the country today, the ethnics are either on the center or to the left of it. Their Irish coreligionists are either close to or just behind the Jews on most measures of liberalism. I do not expect such data to be believed, because too many people have too much emotional energy invested in the opposite opinion. The data, nevertheless, are true.

So the ethnic miracle was accomplished without the complete loss of values and family structures, and without a right-wing backlash either. Indeed it was accomplished without any notable desertion of the Democratic Party. The Stanislowowians and their children and grandchildren made it despite their Polish values and family structure, apparently.

But is the word "despite" appropriate? Might there be a possibility that there was something in the culture of the immigrants that actually facilitated the ethnic miracle?

Preliminary but sophisticated research conducted both at the Department of Labor and the National Bureau of Economic Research (NBER) suggests that Catholics and Jews are more successful in American society than Protestants because of some special factor at work in the early childhood experience of Jewish and Catholic children—perhaps a closer and more intense attention from parents. As Thomas Juster of the NBER observes, "Economists and other social scientists have recently begun to pay close attention to the possible role of preschool investment in children by parents as it affects subsequent educational attainment . . . possible influence on earnings of different amounts of parental time spent with preschool or school-age children. . . . Taking account of family background factors like father's and mother's education and occupation, variables for both Jewish and Catholic religious preference have a significant (positive) impact on reported earnings relative to respondent's reporting of Protestant preference. . . . Plausible hypotheses are that they reflect differences in the cultural background to which the respondents were exposed during formative years or differences in the quality or quantity of parental time inputs."

Not only the Dillingham Commission but even the Protestant ethic has been stood on its head; the familialism of the ethnics, their stubborn differences in family values may well have turned out to be an economic asset. In the absence of further research, such a possibility will remain an intriguing speculation.*

---

*Let it be noted again that while ambition, hard work, and strong family support for achievement may have been the path to upward mobility for the white ethnics, it does not follow that the same path can or must be followed by more recent immigrants. The "ethnic miracle" is worth studying in itself even if it has no pertinence to more recent social problems or provides only useful insights for considering those problems.

All is well then in the ethnic world? Not quite. Their educational mobility is the highest in America, and their income achievement goes beyond what one would expect from people with their education and occupation. However, they do not achieve the occupational status appropriate for their education. On a scale of occupational prestige running from 0 to 99, with the national average 41.8, Italian Catholics, for example, are 2.5 points below the prestige to which their education would entitle them, while British Protestants are 2.2 above the occupational prestige to which their education would entitle them. The ethnics do well, in other words, in converting parental education into their own education, and in converting occupation into income, but they are not nearly so successful in converting education into prestigious occupations.

Interestingly enough, this discrepancy occurs at the upper end of the educational and prestige hierarchies. Poles and Italians do as well in occupational prestige as anyone else if they do not go to college. However, among those who have attended college, Poles, Italians, and even Irish Catholics have notably lower occupational prestige scores. As the accompanying table shows, for those who attended college, the "cost" of being Polish or Italian is almost 40 per cent as high as the cost of being black.

How can one explain this underrepresentation of the college-educated ethnics in the occupational prestige levels to which their education should entitle them? In the past many social scientists would have attributed the difference to a lack of energy or ambition or "need achievement" among the ethnics. However, the considerable economic achievement of the ethnics makes this explanation implausible. Others would suggest that the ethnics are more likely to devote psychic energy to income than to prestigious occupations—to become insurance brokers, for example, instead of college professors. Still others might raise the possibility that in some parts of the country affirmative action programs may have produced costs which the ethnics have had to bear. Whatever the explanation—and much more careful research than is likely to be done

TABLE 1*

*Differences from British Protestants in Occupational
Prestige of Jews and Irish, Italian, and Polish Catholics
by Education (with Blacks for Comparison)*

Ethnic Group (College Graduates Only)	Deviation from British Protestant Average
Irish Catholic	−1.35
Polish Catholic	−4.09
Italian Catholic	−3.93
Jewish	+2.95
Black	−11.04

*Andrew M. Greeley, *Ethnicity, Denomination and Inequality,*
Beverly Hills, Ca.: Sage Publications, Vol. 4, Series No. 90–029,
1976, p. 57.

would be required for certainty—it is a matter of everyday observation that Italian, Polish, and even Irish Catholics are largely absent from the world of the elite private universities, the large foundations, national mass media, the big financial institutions (as opposed to manufacturing corporations), and certain intellectually oriented government agencies. This absence was explained to me once at a national meeting concerned with the lack of women and nonwhite scholars as the result of the "intellectual inferiority produced by Catholic religious belief." Women and blacks, I was informed, are absent because of discrimination, Catholic ethnics because their religion interferes with intellectual achievement. This explanation was offered with a straight face and obvious sincerity.

In fact, since 1960, Catholics have not been underrepresented in those groups pursuing academic careers, finishing dissertations, publishing articles, or even obtaining tenured appointments at the major *state* universities. The myth of Catholic intellectual inferiority simply will not stand up to examination in the light of valid empirical evidence —not at least for Catholics who are under thirty-five, the grandchildren, presumably, of the immigrants. (Given where the eastern and southern European immigrants began, what is surprising is not that their children did not become scholars in proportionate numbers but that their grandchildren did.) If a religio-ethnic group is good enough intellectually to get its young people on the faculties of Michigan, Wisconsin, and California but not quite good enough to make it at Columbia, Yale, Harvard, or the University of Chicago, one begins to wonder what subtle criteria for intellectual excellence are being used at the elite private schools.

There would be very few who would question that the lower scores of the blacks who attended college are the result of discrimination. Unless one can come up with solid evidence for another explanation, intellectual honesty should compel one to take very seriously the possibility that the same explanation should be applied to the lower scores of Polish, Irish, and Italian Catholics. But then it must be noted in all candor that intellectual honesty on the subject of Catholic ethnics is notably absent in many quarters of the elite occupational world in which they seem to be underrepresented.

If there is any ethnic militancy at all, it is not to be found in the vast middle and lower reaches of income and occupational prestige but rather among the ethnic elites, among those college- and graduate school-educated ethnics who bump up against the residual nativism still to be found in the upper strata of American society. It is not the Slovakian steelworkers but the Michael Novaks who are the most likely to be angry ethnics—and with good reason. Or, as far as that goes, it is not the Irish cop or the Irish politician or the Irish attorney who grows angry at elite nativism, for they either do not encounter it or it does not affect them. (The reader may judge for himself whether the author is an angry militant.)

Those of us who stand on the shoulders of the immigrants are ill at ease with our predecessors. Their raw acquisitiveness embarrasses us, and their sacrifices and sufferings cause us pain. It is hard to admit that you owe a great deal to those who came before you. We repress memories of places like the Stanislowowo in the same way we repress memories of such disasters as the Spanish Influenza or the Great Depression; they are too terrible and too close to us for us to be able to think about them very much. It took a long, long time before a movie like *Hester Street* could be made, and it may be another generation or two before the descendants of those brave, strong, ambitious young people who swarmed into this country between 1890 and 1914 will be able to relax sufficiently to place those urban pioneers alongside the other brave people who came over the Appalachian mountains a century earlier to pioneer an unexplored continent. The miracle of the frontier is now a standard part of American mythology. Maybe by the tricentennial, the ethnic miracle will have become one of the respected marvels of the American story.

Origins

The neighborhoods are filled with characters . . .
the old man . . . the crab . . . the kook . . .
the gossip . . . the local poet . . .
and of course the biggest characters of them all, the kids . . .
I know them all, even if I've never met them . . .
So do you . . . most of them are you . . . and me.

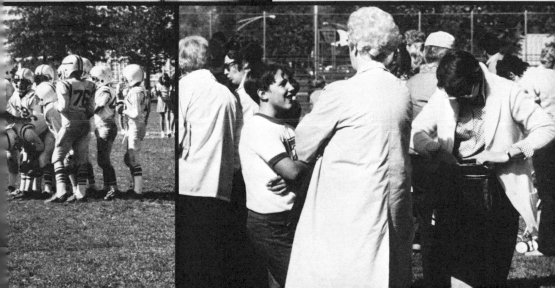

There are two separate but converging reasons why we have neighborhoods. First, we make friends with those with whom we live, and secondly, we live with those who are our friends.

Before I became a sociologist, I always thought that one of the most supercilious, arrogant, and insensitive phrases in the pop sociological literature was "dormitory" suburb. The real action, you see, is in the center of the city, in the world of business, profession, career, finance, occupation. The post–World War II suburbs were merely places where the people who worked in the real world happened to sleep at night and where their women and children happened to live (more recently, for many families, only their children). Now "dormitory suburb" is a smart, clever phrase; but it does not correspond to the reality. The suburbs, even the newest, the rawest, the most uncivilized, are more than just dormitories; they are "home." They are places in which one can escape from the achievement demands of the "real" world and be accepted, more or less, for who one is rather than for what one does. They are places where, for however brief a period of time, the critically important relationships in the lives of professional men and women take place, relationships from which the overwhelmining majority say they receive their principal life satisfactions.

The real world for most workers, indeed, I suspect, even for most professionals, is the place where you work to earn the money which you spend enjoying or attempting to enjoy the good life. Dormitories are not places where one goes for the good life.

Part of the good life is having friends, and humans tend to have their friends living close to them simply because that's the easiest and most convenient place to have them. One cannot emerge from one's apartment or carport every morning and ignore the others who are emerging at the same time. One can hardly tell one's children to avoid all the other children on the block. One can resolutely avoid conversations with neighbors while mowing the lawn or raking the lawn or walking to church, but it takes a major effort. Propinquity increases interaction frequency; and if there are not grounds for hostility, interaction frequency tends to lead to friendship. After all, why not? If you share the same physical space, it is much easier and less strain to be friendly than to be otherwise. One may well be ambivalent about one's neighbors (as I remember, the people next door to us—wherever we lived—were always strange), but it is hard physically to avoid them. Simply for ease of interaction, one pretends to or makes efforts toward close relationships.

One also may have friends a long distance away—the other side of the city, the other end of the country, another part of the planet. But it is inconvenient to see such people. An hour and forty-five minute ride on the expressway system, a transcontinental flight, a week of jet lag are heavy prices to pay to sustain a close relationship; we pay them, but only intermittently. If we are to have friends at all, it's easiest to have them from among our neighbors.

One also, and for roughly similar reasons, develops friendships from among those with whom one works—clients, colleagues, fellow workers. But in the evenings and on the weekends when life *really* takes place, such friends are usually not readily available. Working-time friends tend to be lunch-hour friends; evening and weekend friends tend to be neighbors.

Pop sociologists who write about the mass society and the "transient" individuals within that society would have us believe (for reasons to be seen in a subsequent chapter) that close human relationships may be formed among "autonomous" individuals anywhere almost at random in a manner that is unaffected by such "premodern" factors as land and physical propinquity. It is "progressive" to have close friends all over and "reactionary" or "old fashioned" to have disproportionate numbers of your friends close to that piece of land on which you and your family live.

But such popularizers of the mass society dispense all too easily with geography. One may have instant communication and quick transportation, but it still requires time to traverse space, and if you are traversing it during rush hour, it may well take as much time now as it did before the automobile. And an hour-and-a-half drive when the party breaks up at 11:30 is an ordeal even for "modern" humans who pride themselves on autonomy and mobility.

One need not postulate any territorial imperative about it. People simply get attached to the place where they live; it is familiar, comfortable in its familiarity (whatever its inconveniences may be), and it's yours. To defend it one need not assume an aggressive instinct but only common sense. To form close alliances with people who share the same piece of turf is merely a matter of geographical convenience and common interest. There may be physiological and deep psychological dynamisms at work, but one need not postulate them to explain the rather quick emergence of intensive interaction networks among people who live close to one another. The pertinent question is not why territorial behavior continues even into the "modern" world (which is, I think, the mystery with which Robert Ardrey wrestles) but why anyone thought that it wouldn't continue. Just try to ignore the man who barbecues next door of a summer evening, or the parents of your child's best friend down the block, or the woman who weeds her garden next to yours just across the fence. Local community is natural and human beings seek it because they like each other.

There are, of course, both impersonal environments and impersonal people. The high-rise apartment building is spatially and geographically maladapted for easy community formation. Still, many people in high-rise apartments do manage to develop rather intense interaction networks. There are also people who prefer privacy; they are probably disproportionately attracted to apartment house living and may avoid contact with their neighbors; all they want is for people to leave them alone. Sometimes such a passionate defense of one's own privacy is offensive, especially to the frantic and fanatic "neighboring" that goes on in some of the newer suburban communities. The older neighborhoods usually had enough different types around that eccentricity was tolerated if not appreciated. A devoted misanthrope was usually left alone.

But there is a strong predisposition in most humans to be gregarious, and "industrialization" and "modernization," far from eliminating "neighboring," as some of the theorists of the mass society would have us believe, provide more time, more occasion and more resources for it, and a much more sophisticated vocabulary for talking about it. It is, in other words, virtually impossible to prevent most people from setting up close interaction networks among those who live close to them.

We also tend to live where our friends live. A denizen of the mass society may pick up the Sunday paper and carefully and rationally select what looks like the best real estate buys and then go out with a cool, calculating eye and make the sort of deal Adam Smith would have been proud of. But a large number of people rely on informal communication networks to find out about available housing opportunities precisely where friends or other members of the family already live. The presence of friends and family facilitates becoming part of a new community and also one can get an advance intelligence report from friends and family about what the community is like.

In the movie *Hester Street,* the wife asked, "But Yankel, in New York where are the gentiles?"

The Jewish immigrants came to Delancey Street and Hester Street and the other streets of the Lower East Side because that's where the other Jewish immigrants were—their friends, their relatives, their acquaintances. Where else would one go? There may have been a few brave souls who were willing to face the new world all alone, but most immigrants sought out the places where there were people they knew or places that had been recommended to them by those who purported to know about them. As the numbers of a given group increased, their concentration in a given neighborhood, the community services to cater to the group's specific needs began to develop—kosher meat markets, small synagogues, coffee shops, for example, in the Hester Street environment. And the presence of these services reinforced the attractiveness of the community for yet newer waves of immigrants, who would go through the painful and confusing experience of being a "greenhorn" in the relatively protected environment of the neighborhood which, while it was far different from the world they had left behind, still had more in common with that world than did the

America beyond the boundaries of the neighborhood.

As I pointed out in an earlier chapter, the concentrations of specific ethnic groups in these neighborhoods were not so exclusive as they seemed to the immigrants and as retrospective myth has made them. I suspect there were gentiles on Hester Street, or if not there precisely, a block or two or three away from it. According to the mythology, however, propagated by the Chicago School and its disciples, these heavy ethnic concentrations tended to break up as the ethnic groups became more assimilated to American life. From the point of view of the Chicago School, such a change was both necessary and desirable, as well as inevitable. The cultural inferiority and the social disorganization of the immigrants may well have made their clustering together in immigrant entry ports understandable and, in the short run, beneficial; but as they became more and more "American" and gave up the premodern values they brought with them from the plains of Poland and the hills of Sicily, the immigrants or their children or their grandchildren could be expected to behave like modern, rational, scientific Americans and base their choice of neighborhood on logical decisions a consideration of income, education, or occupation would impel.

Doubtless ethnic concentrations in certain communities have diminished since 1910, but they have not diminished nearly so much as the assimilationist model would have us believe. And they have not diminished at all in the last several decades. A number of recent very careful social researchers such as Nathan Kantrowitz, Abraham Guest, James A. Weed, Gordon A. Darroch, and William G. Marstin have demonstrated that indices of segregation continue to be very high among white ethnic groups in urban America. Indeed, Kantrowitz points out that if blacks were white in skin color, the "segregation index" between blacks and whites would diminish from .8 to only about .6.

The "segregation index" is a measure of what proportion of two populations would have to be shifted around in order that the population might be equally distributed in the area units which are the subject of the analysis. It is a measure of relative concentration instead of absolute concentration. Thus if there is a high segregation index between Swedes and Danes in New York City (and it is above .5), it does not mean that there are some all-Swedish or all-Danish neighborhoods but that Swedes tend to be concentrated in some neighborhoods and Danes in others, and one would have to move around more than half of the population of these two groups to have them evenly distributed in the analytic areas. Interestingly enough, while the indices of segregation continue to be high—even between Polish and Italian Catholics or between German and Irish Catholics—in the big cities, indices of centralization or decentralization show little variation among the different white ethnic groups. The Chicago School was right up to a point: the ethnics did tend to move out of the old inner city toward the fringes and the suburbs, so they are no longer concentrated in inner-city neighborhoods. But they did not move out of the inner city randomly; on the contrary, the typical move seems to be to the next neighborhood out and then to the next neighborhood beyond that. Indices of centralization, then, for the individual groups are low but indices of segregation between the various groups are high.

Such sociological talk may confuse the reader until he stops to think of a street like Milwaukee Avenue in Chicago. At one time the Poles were heavily concentrated in a few neighborhoods close to the center of the city, some of which clustered around Milwaukee Avenue. Now they are strung out along Milwaukee Avenue to the fringes of the city and into the suburbs. Milwaukee Avenue is still a Polish street; no neighborhood has the heavy concentration that the Stanislowowo did in 1910, but virtually all the neighborhoods along that avenue are disproportionately Polish. Not all Poles in Chicago live near Milwaukee Avenue (or similar "Polish corridors") and not everyone along Milwaukee Avenue is Polish, but you are still more likely to find Poles living in the Milwaukee Avenue area than you are elsewhere; and the probability of their living in neighborhoods along Milwaukee Avenue has apparently not changed appreciably since 1950.

The Chicago School was right about the ethnics moving out of the old neighborhoods; it was wrong, however, to think that they would move as individuals. They moved as groups, as communities, indeed as neighborhoods. In some cases, one almost feels that a whole neighborhood pulled up stakes and moved a mile or two further out. Certainly Beverly, my favorite neighborhood, was put together from a number of such moves by substantial segments of people at almost the same time.

Guest and Weed conclude their article by suggesting the possibility that ethnic communities may have begun to stabilize in American society and that the patterns of ethnic residential segregation will continue for some time to come—for several generations, they suggest —at about the 1960–1970 level. In other words, the tendency to live among your own when "your own" is defined on the basis of religio-ethnicity has survived the immigration experience, and it persists in American society and is likely to persist at the present levels for the foreseeable future. There may be no ethnically homogenous neighborhoods; there never were. But ethnic concentrations in certain areas continue to exist and will continue to do so. The assimilation model, in other words, is knocked into a cocked hat.

Does it follow then that Americans choose their homes, at least in part, on the basis of the ethnic concentration in a particular neighborhood? I would suggest that that is not the case for most people. They choose their homes in areas relatively close to where they lived before and where families and friends tend to live; they also choose neighborhoods by the availability of community services which they have grown up to believe are important (synagogues, parochial schools, art centers, and so forth). Without reflecting much on the ethnic composition of a neighborhood, they end up more likely to live in neighborhoods with their own kind. If you ask them whether they had been "looking" for an Italian, Polish, or Irish neighborhood, they may deny it; what they were looking for was a neighborhood in which they would feel comfortable. For a number of conscious and unconscious reasons, it often happens to be a neighborhood where a substantial number of their own kind live.

But it is said that there is so much mobility in American society that people nowadays don't often stay in the cities in which they grew up.

There is much mobility in the United States, of course; people do move from city to city or from town to city or from one part of a large city to another. But in fact the majority of Americans are relatively stable in their spatial locations. Thus in a study of Chicago neighborhoods conducted by my colleagues Kathleen McCourt and David Greenstone, more than two-thirds of those interviewed had been born in Chicago and more than three-fifths were not planning to move out of the neighborhood in which they lived. Only one-third of those who were thinking of moving said they would move out of the Chicago metropolitan area. Thirty-eight per cent of the Catholics and 25 per cent of the Protestants had relatives living in the same neighborhood; more than seven-tenths said they liked the neighborhood; and more than three-fifths said they had many neighbors who were friends. One-quarter of the Catholics and 16 per cent of the Protestants said that more than half of their close friends lived in the neighborhood.

Despite "modernization" and "industrialization" and all the other things that have happened, many people, probably the majority, have strong ties to neighborhood and to locality. They are reluctant to give them up. If career or job forces them to, they will live with strangers; if given their preference, they will live with their own kind.

So we make friends of those we live with and we like to live with those who are our friends. This is the source of neighborhood feeling. It may not be rational or "modern" but it is eminently human.

I have always been struck by the eagerness with which Catholics announce that the age of the neighborhood is over, or that the neighborhood isn't as important as it used to be, or that the new suburbs aren't neighborhoods. Recently, in a generally pro-neighborhood statement, the National Council of Catholic Bishops allowed that the neighborhoods were declining in importance in American society. They advanced no evidence for such an assertion, but then if you are a Catholic bishop in the United States, you don't need any evidence for any assertion you care to make. We have seen that the sociological evidence indicates neighborhoods are not declining in importance and that residential concentrations of Catholic ethnic groups have not changed appreciably in at least twenty years. The bishops think differently, perhaps, because "everyone" knows that neighborhoods are declining and that is that.

Some Catholics are eager to write off the neighborhoods because they have accepted the conventional wisdom that the neighborhood is nonrational and premodern. Having just been "liberated" from the Catholic ghetto and feeling themselves candidates for membership in the nation's intellectual and cultural elites, Catholics must really prove themselves. They must demonstrate that they are no longer attached to the nonrational and premodern values of their immigrant past; and so, more eagerly and insistently than the others, they keep repeating the magic words "neighborhoods aren't important any more." It makes for good conversation with their neighbors at cocktail parties.

Another good conversation topic at such gatherings is whether the suburb is a neighborhood at all. Of course, some suburbs are quite indistinguishable from neighborhoods. I think of Evanston and Cicero, outside Chicago, and Beverly, suburban in its culture, inside. Other newer suburban communities have not yet developed the familiar local institutions that reinforce and bind together neighborhood ties. But the pertinent researchable question is not whether suburbs are neighborhoods but to what extent neighborhood behavior continues in a suburban environment. When phrased that way, one is forced to conclude, it seems to me, that "neighboring"—that is to say, social interaction with one's neighbors—is if anything more intense in many of the new upper-middle-class suburbs than it was in the old working-class and lower-middle-class urban communities. A suburb for many people is a self-conscious, deliberate, and explicit attempt to create an even more intense local community than existed in the old neighborhood. It may lack the richness, the diversity, the flexibility, and what in retrospect could be called the "color" of the old neighborhood, but such characteristics may develop in time. The "one-class" professional suburb may be more dreary and monotonous than the variegated ethnic urban community, but on the basis of the available research evidence, as well as impressions of lots of suburbanites, its residents are certainly not less intense in their propensity to "neighbor."

Two other points must be made about the origins of neighborhoods. First of all the very word "neighborhood" can have a number of different if related meanings. It can stand for "my block," the "couple of blocks around us," "this part of the parish," "my parish," or "the whole general area around here." We slip back and forth in daily usage from one meaning to another in part because the meanings, like the space they represent, tend to overlap. There is no confusion in this in daily usage because we are quickly cued into a context of the meaning the other person is attaching to the word. One of the problems of much neighborhood research is that it has not comprehended the great flexibility of the word itself and not tried to seek out the various usages to which respondents put the word. One research project concluded that there were no such things as neighborhoods because people were not able to agree on or even clearly define the boundaries of a community. However, communities can certainly exist and be very important in people's lives even if they have only the vaguest notion of what the outer limits of the community are. The boundaries become quite specific, however, if one has to operationalize what a given sense of what neighborhood means to him. Thus for those with young children, an obvious and perhaps primary sense of the word "neighborhood" is that area within which one feels it is safe to commit one's children to play. If a survey interviewer asked that kind of question, a clear and specific delineation of boundaries would almost certainly be given by the respondent.

It is not true to say that because "neighborhood" means many things it means nothing to people. Its core meaning is "the area where I live," and the definition of that area expands and contracts depending upon what aspect of life one is talking about. In this book neighborhood is understood to mean "this general area around here"—a more extensive definition than is used in most ordinary discussion. However, it should be rememberd that even in the broad sense of "the area around here," the neighborhood still shares the strong emotional investment which is involved in the "our block" definition of the term because things that are seen to affect the general area are seen as affecting the block.

Neighborhoods are different from each other. They differ in their architecture, their geography, in the nature and the permeability of their boundaries, their physical location, in the community services that are available, the education, income, and occupation of those who live in them. Neighborhoods tend to have "personalities" all their own, and while it is hard to define such an attribute to outsiders, those who have lived in different neighborhoods have little doubt that the personalities change from neighborhood to neighborhood. The mix and blend of ethnic groups, for example, can have a considerable impact on the culture of a community—especially since those who founded the immigrant parishes for the various ethnic groups had rather different ideas about what they were doing.

The Irish immigrants, clergy and laity, without much self-conscious reflection about it, continued to do what they had done in the rural villages of Ireland. Once the parish church was put up, it automatically became the center of things. Why would one expect anything different? However, the Resurrectionist Fathers, who were the most vigorous and outspoken leaders of the Polish immigrant community, operated on a much more explicit, detailed, and self-conscious program. The community-parish (of the sort we see in the Stanislowowo and its environs) was a matter of explicit Resurrectionist philosophy and detailed in their articles and books. They built the big Polish cathedrals along Milwaukee Avenue precisely because the steeples of those cathedrals would bring back the memories of those that dominated the towns from which the immigrants had come. They strove to recreate Polish community because there seemed to be no other way to preserve the faith, and because the Resurrectionist Fathers were also Polish patriots, the preservation of Polish community in the United States ensured continuing support and pressure for a free and independent Poland. The conflict between the "clericals" of St. Stan's and the "nationalists" at the church down the street, Holy Trinity, was largely over how one was to maintain the delicate balance between being

Catholic and being Polish while at the same time being American.

The Italian clergy, in particular the Calabrini Fathers, had yet another model. Since Italy was essentially a one-religion country, its religion and culture stood in easier and more relaxed relationship with one another there than in many of the other countries from which the immigrants came. The maintenance of Italian religious loyalty involved a continuation of a much more relaxed and casual Italian approach to religion in the United States—much to the horror of the (to the Italian view) rigid, Irish Catholic pastors who actually expected people to go to church every Sunday to prove that they were Christians. Parish loyalty, church attendance, the parish as a hyperactive center of the community were less important in the Italian neighborhood than the maintenance of critically important religious symbols such as feast days and festivals. In the Italian style of religious affiliation, the ties of family life were such that one really didn't have to worry very much about "community." One could take that for granted and turn to other matters such as resisting the cultural incursions of the (as they were perceived) rigid, judicially minded Irish clergy. (Which only served to infuriate the Irish. More than one Irish priest was heard to exclaim in frustration, "Who the hell wrote canon law anyway?")

The Czech parish emerged from yet another matrix—the formation of voluntary associations, mostly religious, in nineteenth-century Czech villages as a response to the changing shape of the Czech agricultural economy. These voluntary associations equipped the immigrants with the skills they needed to found similar associations when they arrived in America. As Josef Barton comments, "Families gathered into voluntary associations lent their energies to the construction of churches, schools, and orphanages, those standard features of urban Catholicism."* Coming from a Europe where they had already begun to create new styles of community life, the Czech immigrants already had a communal sense, a capacity to respond to collective needs. The Czech

*Josef Barton, "Religion and Cultural Change in Czech Immigrant Communities," unpublished manuscript, p. 19.

laity, in other words, formed their communities for themselves and invited the church to come in.

We must await further research like Barton's to see whether other European groups developed similarly their styles of community in this country. Certainly both Polish and Lithuanian immigrants organized their own religious associations and often invited the church to provide them with a priest. But one has the impression that the Czech families and associations were much more independent and less likely to yield to clerical domination than other immigrant groups.

One can find at least four different styles of neighborhood-building in the Irish, Polish, Italian, and Czech immigrant groups. There are doubtless more. But comparative study of ethnic neighborhoods can only seriously begin when we have much better and more systematic knowledge than we do now about the emergence of the neighborhood as a distinctive form of urban life. But such knowledge in its turn will require a generation of scholars like Josef Barton who think that ethnic neighborhoods are worth studying in vast and passionate detail.

And such people had better not try to get jobs at Catholic universities.

Nonetheless, the young historians and sociologists work away, unmindful that it is "not modern" to be interested in neighborhoods. Dominic Pacyga, for example, describes how the supposedly conservative "back of the yards" community in Chicago rose against the mounted police who tried to break (and finally did, with the aid of the courts) a strike.

> ... the women took the most radical and violent stand in the strike. They were among the first to confront the police, throwing red pepper into the eyes of the horses and the mounted police. Other tactics were used to stop motorcycle police. The children of the neighborhood spread tacks up and down Ashland Avenue in an attempt to puncture the tires of the motorcycle police. Those workers who did not strike often found mobs of strikers in front of their houses chanting and throwing bricks, sometimes starting fires.
>
> A small park located near 43rd and Ashland, called Davis Square, was

the scene of rioting. The rioters charged the police, calling them Cossacks and pelting them with bottles and bricks.*

One can hardly imagine the peaceful back of the yards community today as a place where there were once radical riots. Davis Square hardly looks like a historic location in the history of the American labor movement. Few lakeshore liberals acknowledge that radical outbursts like the American Railroad strike, the Pullman strike, the Little Steel strike, and even the Haymarket riot (most of whose participants were Polish and Irish) were to a very considerable extent neighborhood uprisings.

It is the diversity of neighborhoods which gives urban life its variety, a variety which is necessarily invisible for judges, administrators, planners, bureaucrats, and professors who have become the neighborhood's enemies. If a human institution is "premodern," nonrational, old-fashioned, superstitious, illogical, particularistic, and ethnic, how can it possibly contribute anything to urban life? If one is to have a peaceful, happy, healthy city, one needs not diversity and variety but homogenization; for a bland, undifferentiated city is the modern, scientific, rational city.

Call it Orange County.

*Dominic Pacyga, "A Neighborhood's Radical Response to Industrial Conditions: The Chicago Packinghouse Strike of 1921," a paper presented at the annual meeting of the Northern Illinois and Wisconsin chapter of the Association of American Studies, March 13, 1976, pp. 13–14.

6

The Enemies
of Neighborhoods

Some neighborhoods don't make it . . .
and some historic buildings . . . like old St. Columbkille's,
the pride of the immigrant Irish, abandoned by
a foolish archdiocese with no respect for its past . . .
blight, decay, destruction . . . the results of ignorance,
malice, greed, stupidity.

If the neighborhood is such a "natural" community and if so many of us have such pleasant memories of the neighborhoods of our past, why is our society bent on destroying them? Why do the administrators, the planners, the scholars, the federal judges, the journalists, the high-level thinkers all either actively oppose the neighborhood or advocate policies which will certainly lead to neighborhood destruction?

It is a mistake, for example, to see the controversy over busing as having to do principally with improving educational opportunities of blacks. The evidence that busing does no such thing is too powerful for anyone to have any illusions. Busing is a deliberate, self-conscious, and explicit attempt to destroy the neighborhood school because it is, in principle, racist. Indeed, in principle, neighborhoods are racist, and if you manage to destroy the neighborhood school, sure enough, the neighborhood itself soon begins to crumble. Which of course proves exactly what the pro-busing forces want to prove: people who live in the neighborhood are racists.

Make no mistake about it, the assumption is irrefutable and unanswerable. Support for the neighborhood schools equals racism. Even to raise the subject in the presence of a group of college professors (most of whose children are in a private school) is to risk being denounced out of hand. Neighborhood schools are beyond discussion; they are simply bad. Even those blacks who want to have neighborhood schools of their own must be dissuaded from doing so, because without realizing it they are cooperating in white racism by wanting schools of their own. Indeed, some members of the elites would go so far as to want to see the Catholic inner-city schools closed because such schools provide an alternative educational system for black parents to enable them to choose high quality all-black schools over low quality and dangerous integrated schools.

But the attack on the neighborhood schools is only one part, and a small part at that, of the determined effort to destroy the neighborhood by those who run our distressed society. Urban renewal, expressway construction, mammoth concentrated high-rise housing projects, a dual real estate market, redlining, the creation of lily-white suburbs through the legal fiction of city boundaries, the dumping of the welfare poor on certain neighborhoods are all deliberate attempts to destroy neighborhoods. And it matters not whether the attempts are made by the left in opposition to the neighborhood school or by the right in such practices as redlining and the dual real estate market or by the nonideological government technocrats in their city-planning and welfare-dumping activities.

It has been almost two decades since Jane Jacobs and almost one decade since school decentralization in New York City. We know all about Robert Moses, we have had hundreds, perhaps thousands, of Alinsky-type organizations; and still the steady destruction of urban neighborhoods continues unabated. One has to assume that at this late date such destruction is deliberate. Those who are out to destroy the neighborhoods may not be explicit in their intentions or even completely aware of what they are doing; nonetheless, their basic premises and assumptions about urban life are such that they will necessarily do everything they can to destroy them. For the neighborhoods stand for everything these people think is unspeakable and intolerable in modern life.

I have been in the priesthood long enough now to have seen several generations of young priests arrive on the scene and repeat the cliches of their predecessors about how they were going to create community organizations in their neighborhoods and preserve them from destruction. They are totally unaware, it is to be feared, that they are only parroting the same vague hopes, the same unperceptive cliches, the same shallow populism of those who went before them; and they have gone down to the same defeat. You cannot defend the neighborhood at the neighborhood level; you have got to change the policies of urban society at the level of city, state, and national government.

There have appeared new, more militant, and more sophisticated community organizations and community coalitions on the scene recently. I was profoundly skeptical of those kinds of organizations in the past because they seemed to be little more than fronts for the radical activists who staffed them and who used neighborhood people in their social revolution game. Indeed, I regret to say from my observations inside the Alinsky-type organization movements, that the staffs almost invariably manipulated the neighborhood folk for their own political purposes. The famous national columnist Nicholas von Hoffman was one of the most slippery and notorious of the neighborhood manipulators in the first Alinsky days. The professional staffs of activist organizations all too frequently were in fact agents of the enemy because they approached the neighborhoods with fundamentally the same kinds of values as those who would destroy them. But the new activist organizations like CAP (Citizens Against Pollution) and MAHA (Metropolitan Area Housing Alliance) in Chicago seem more honest and ready to learn from ordinary people instead of indoctrinating their members. Yet the tasks they face are immense. They need all the help—and all the luck—they can get.

For the city planners the neighborhood is an is an obstacle to their elegant schemes; for the redlining bankers, the neighborhood is an obstacle to their greed; and for some of the community organizers, the neighborhood is a tool to obtain political power. None of them, however, is prepared to concede that the neighborhood is a good thing in itself. They cannot do so, I will argue in this book, because their values and their assumptions say that it is not. The assumptions, the premises, the values, the fundamental philosophy of those who govern and administer and finance and plan our cities are anti-neighborhood. The elites simply cannot comprehend why anyone with any intelligence and sophistication should care about neighborhoods. If forced to yield here and there to neighborhood strength, they will do so; but thus far, they have not been forced to rethink their assumptions, to toss their basic premises out the window. Until that happens, the neighborhood people may draw a winning card now and then, but they will still have the urban deck stacked against them.

I am often asked if I favor a policy of protecting and preserving neighborhoods much as the upper-class do-gooders support the protection and preservation of architectural landmarks and endangered species. The thought is intriguing, but most of those who are concerned about old buildings are notably unconcerned about people, and especially about semipermanent networks of human relationships (which is all a neighborhood is). A man named David Lowe did a book some time ago about "lost Chicago," an account of all the beautiful architectural gems that had been thoughtlessly leveled by us bad folk who live in Chicago. Lowe's book is written in white-hot anger at the depravity of Chicagoans in destroying so many beautiful buildings. I am not unsympathetic with Lowe's concerns, though I am affronted by the paranoid tone of his book. A city must be concerned about its great architecture (though I confess I fail to see that Mrs. Potter Palmer's mansion is great architecture—at best a curiosity, I think). But it must balance its need for growth and economic opportunities for its people with its need to preserve important architecture. The balance is not easy to maintain nor are the decisions involved self-evident. In all his outrage about the destroyed Stock Exchange, Garrick Theatre, and other landmarks, Mr. Lowe shows not the slightest awareness that the city also destroyed some of its most vivid, original, fascinating, and historically valuable neighborhoods. I guess I think that "Greek town" in Chicago was a hell of a lot more interesting and more important than Mrs. Potter Palmer's mansion. The point of view that holds physical constructions to be more valuable to preserve than constructions of human networks is irrelevant if not positively dangerous. The self-styled "independents" in Chicago politics will flail out at the mayor for the destruction of "Greek town" and the partial destruction of the Italian neighborhood around Taylor Street, but there is nothing in their other actions to suggest that they do so for any other reason than to make political points. They can lament the passing of the Stock Exchange and the Garrick Theatre and ignore the obliteration of Woodlawn, Englewood, and other neighborhoods in Chicago with complete ease of conscience and intellectual consistency. In their view of things buildings are to be preserved and neighborhoods allowed to go. They lamented the passing of a neighborhood only when Richard J. Daley was to be blamed for it.

I don't advocate a national park or national monument approach to neighborhoods, though I do think that some communities ought to be preserved as part of explicit and conscious national policy because they are a lot more interesting than South Dakota grasslands, for example. Ideally the neighborhood should be able to survive on its own, and if there are not the social and human resources to keep it going, then the neighborhood should not require subsidies to keep it alive. One does not ask of a government active support for neighborhoods, merely neutrality.

The problem is not so much that neighborhoods need government support as that they need to be free from implacable government opposition. One begs the government to give the neighborhoods a fighting chance, to abandon the tactics and the strategies that inevitably—and in some sense intentionally—are designed to obliterate neighborhoods.

The Taylor Street community still manages to exist. The north end was cut off by an expressway, the east end by a great ugly, evil university campus, the south end by an equally ugly public housing construction. Still, Taylor Street drew back and continues to exist. The schools at Notre Dame of Chicago and Our Lady of Pompeii are filled, the Vernon Park Tap (one of the finest restaurants in Chicago) is still open, new home construction continues, and, as one enthusiastic Taylor Street denizen said to me, "We got a great neighborhood—Italians and blacks and students and professors. What could be more American?" But the destruction of a good segment of the Taylor Street community to build the University of Illinois Chicago campus was one of the worst misfortunes of Richard J. Daley's administration. It was a mistake made with good intent. Daley knew Chicago needed a state university campus, that the children of ethnic families (white and black and brown) who would go to that university had to have ready access to public transportation so they could go to their afternoon and evening jobs after morning classes. The "circle" (the coming together of the major expressways) seemed to be the ideal place; indeed, it was virtually the only place for such construction. Balancing on the one hand the good of preserving a neighborhood and on the other the good of providing college education for the ethnic children of Chicago, Daley reluctantly chose the latter. I doubt that any other serious political leader in his position would have done any differently. Those who try to score political points against him were unable to name an alternative site for the campus—and many of them never gave a damn whether the children of ethnics ever got an education or not.

The mayor's mistake was to permit the educational bureaucrats and the hack architects who work for them to persuade him that the only way to build a university campus is to level a neighborhood. Administrators and their architect flunkies have only one model of campus construction: empty land and monolithic buildings. I think they might have spotted throughout the Taylor Street community (probably at lower cost) a number of smaller, decentralized buildings and even gone so far as to rehabilitate some of the existing community buildings. To erect a university campus which would not be merely physically located in the city but actually integrated with the neighborhood of the city would have enabled the students to walk up and down the streets of the neighborhood, mingling with other people and bringing not destruction but new life and vitality to the community. The chancellor of the campus, of course, would not be able to stand in his skyscraper office and survey the vast domain that he rules; he, too, might have to walk the streets with his students and neighbors. But you don't build universities *in* neighborhoods; you tear down the neighborhoods and then put the universities on the empty space. Who has reason to think any differently? That's the way it has always been done, isn't it?

The mayor should have told his planners to go to hell and build the university in the Taylor Street community and disrupt it as little as possible in the process. But like so many Americans, it is to be feared, he was (at that time, at any rate) so bemused by the power and the magic of professional educators that he took everything they said as gospel truth. The crowning irony is that the fools who run the University of Illinois Circle Campus and teach in it have steadfastly ignored both the city and the city administration since they got their huge, ugly campus put up. They are in the city, all right, but they are not of it. And that's the way things were designed to work from the beginning.

Another interesting example of what the elites can do to a neighborhood was an attempt by television commentator Bill Moyers to do a program on a threatened community in Long Island (threatened with racial integration). The words Moyers spoke were profoundly sympathetic to the beleaguered people in the community, but the pictures his cameramen and directors took were violently against the community. The black couple chosen were literate, idealistic, appealing; the white neighborhood types were ugly, stupid, inarticulate, barely literate. The black search for a better life in a good community was presented sympathetically; the white dilemma of racial immigration destroying the community was treated caustically, and except for one quick shot of another neighborhood which had changed several years before (and turned into a nearly abandoned slum) there were no images or pictures at all of what the neighbors feared. One saw a chilling sequence in which white children chased a little black girl out of a playground, but, of course, one saw no pictures of black teenagers using knives to extort money from white teenagers in the high school. Nor was one told, incidentally, that a number of other black families had moved into the community without any opposition before the militant couple about whom the documentary was made had arrived on the scene. In other words, even when our elite commentators like Bill Moyers try to be fair and objective in their presentations of the plight of neighborhoods, they can't quite bring it off. Their intellectual and moral blinders are such that they have got to slant the case against the inhabitants of the neighborhood.*

Furthermore, if one looks at what passes for urban higher education (in places like the great UICC), one finds that so far as the faculty and administration have any concerns other than maintaining their own power and budgets and promoting their own careers, they view the principal goal of their educational activities as the deracination and the

---

*Nor is it necessarily a case of black against white, as the Moyers' documentary tried to make it appear. Black ethnics are at least as strong in their support of neighborhood communities as whites, and have even more to suffer when the welfare poor are "dumped" on them and *their* communities begin to deteriorate.

alienation of the young people from their neighborhoods. If you get a bright, articulate young Italian or Pole or Puerto Rican or black, the way to educate him is to turn him against the values of his family, his friends, his community; for only the isolated, alienated, deracinated individual in modern society is truly mobile and educated (by which they mean, of course, he is a good candidate for graduate school and for the academic life). As academies for the graduate schools, the undergraduate schools must deracinate as many young people as possible, because only the alienated and the isolated can be truly dispassionate, objective, and rational research scholars. The goal of higher education is *not* to enable a person to look with critical sympathy and sympathetic criticism on his own assumptions and those of the people who raised him but to turn him against those assumptions. Education can be a liberating experience not by making you conscious of who you are and where you come from but by turning you into a rebel, an adversary, an implacable enemy of everything which your family and community stood for.

Such a pedagogy is psychologically dangerous and educationally absurd. But it is still what higher education is, and if it fails to achieve its goals it is not for lack of trying.

But why should one view with equanimity the passing of neighborhoods? Why is it considered absurd that an institution of higher education should be integrated into the neighborhood? Why should one rejoice at the deracination of a bright young kid from the neighborhood?

I have argued through this chapter that such goals are a matter of conscious and explicit intent on the part of our intellectual and cultural elites. I do *not* mean that they have national conferences on the subject or that they explicitly set it out as one of the goals of social policy. I mean rather that the perspectives from which the elites view human life in society is such that they cannot help but think that neighborhoods are old fashioned, reactionary, particularistic, and inferior. Within such a frame of reference, they are certainly not going to try to protect neighborhoods from destruction or to adjust their social policies to preserve them. On the contrary, they will be simply incapable of understanding why anyone with any intelligence and good will would want to preserve a neighborhood. Hence, when the calculations are made for social policy decisions, neighborhood preservation becomes a totally unimportant variable. It is the cheapest cost one must bear, and if you fall to the bottom of the urban agenda these days, you've had it. The elites, therefore, are bent on neighborhood destruction precisely because they see no reason why neighborhood preservation should not be put at the very bottom of the urban agenda. They know full well that the neighborhoods will rot there. They shrug their shoulders and say, "So what?"

The word "modern" summarizes the answer. What is modern is good, what is not modern is bad. Neighborhoods, alas, are not modern.

Much of our attitudes and behavior is regulated by imagery in our preconscious. We have a set of "pictures" or, to use a fancier word, "symbols" which enable us to organize and shape the experience of our daily life and to respond to that experience. And in that process we shape the very world we experience. These pictures or images describe both the way the world is (and thus are descriptive) and also, sometimes, they describe the way the world ought to be (and thus become normative). We sometimes talk about these images and they become ideas or, to use social science language, "models." But normally, they are implicit, unself-conscious, taken for granted. For that reason they can be very powerful indeed; they affect what we look at, how we look at it, and how we interpret what we see. They are usually beyond discussion or argument; they are deeply held convictions and they are challenged at the risk of conflict—internal certainly and often external. They are more than just convictions that appeal to the intellect; there is color, sound, feel, and taste to these images, which gives them a powerful emotional appeal and a compelling moral force.

One such image is the "melting pot" idea, which for many Americans is the only way to cope with the diversity and pluralism in our society. The diversity is there all right, the melting pot picture says, but it's going away. We must tolerate those who are different from us for the time being, but in the years to come, through better education and increasing distance from their lands of origin, they will lose their foreign ways and become like us. So the elimination of ethnic pluralism in American society, according to the melting pot model, is an inevitable ongoing process that is not only the way things are but also the way things should be.

Now the melting pot image is offended by neighborhoods because they seem to be a residue of ethnic pluralism. Worse than that, neighborhoods offend a much more comprehensive image of which the melting pot is merely a development; and that is the image of "modernization." We begin to learn about it very early in our educational careers, and we absorb it from our schools, our families, from the mass media, even from serious scholarly research. It is virtually an unchallengeable assumption in a social science, and even scholars whose findings run contrary to the modernization picture still feel constrained to invoke the picture when describing their findings. Small wonder, because it was out of the idea of modernization, expressed by such scholars as Durkheim, Weber, Comte, Tonnies, that modern social science was born. To abandon it would mean to abandon one of the most important props of the emotional and intellectual life of most of America's intelligentsia, and indeed a large number of ordinary citizens.

There are three steps to the modernization picture: change, evolution, progress. Obviously, many things have changed since the Second World War, since the First World War, since the turn of the century, since our grandparents' day, since our family emigrated from Europe. This change also seems to represent an evolutionary development from a primitive to a less primitive style of life; we live longer, we eat better, we are more protected from disease, and have richer and fuller lives. So there has been change, and it seems to be in an evolutionary direction, and it seems to represent progress. Things are getting better and better. Who can fight that?

Now some people are fighting it because they see that the costs of industrialization, for example, are so high in air, water, land pollution, destruction of the environment, and the alienation of man from nature. Such people generally have a very rosy and romantic notion of what life was like before the industrial revolution produced material affluence and longer life. Half of us would not have lived to our twenty-fifth birthdays and few of us would have seen fifty. But even the ecological reactionaries who want to return to older harmonies with nature take for granted not merely the industrial and scientific revolution but also —and here's the rub—that something fundamental has changed about human life.

It was, you see, not merely that our ancestors had less schooling than we did and that they lived shorter and less comfortable lives than we do; they were much more prone to disease and much more easily wiped out by famine, plague, physical breakdowns; they found it less easy to move around their physical environment and communicate at great distances. It is not merely that they lacked our scientific and technical resources, it is also true, argue the modernists, that they had different values, different life styles, and different aspirations than we do.

They were tribal; the land they worked was held in common, they lived as part of extended families (many with several generations together), their primary loyalty was to the family and the clan, they were superstitious, their marriages were arranged by their parents, they were ruled by sacred, hierarchical authority (a holy church or a holy king), they were bound psychically and legally as well as physically to the land, they probably could not read or write. Their lives were dull, nasty, brutish, and short.

But with the Protestant Reformation and the Renaissance and later the industrial revolution, humankind broke away from all the old ties and became modern, autonomous, mobile, independent, enlightened, rational, scientific. To summarize how it all happened, I have set up in tabular form seven descriptive propositions that are a sort of synthesis of the modernization model as one will find it in many writings of modern social scientists. Alongside each description is its concomitant normative proposition which is vigorously rejected by the "modernists."

Mind you, this model is not only a description of what has happened since the Reformation, the Renaissance, or the industrial revolution; it is the way things ought to be. It is not only change, it is inevitable evolutionary change, and it is also progress. (How can one have change without progress? ask the modernization enthusiasts.)

Yet there is very little evidence to support the modernization model, and in fact, much of the evidence that does exist runs to the contrary. A typical family in preindustrial Europe was nuclear, not extended; the typical farm was not a tribal commune but a single-family farm; in many places in the premodern world, marriages were a matter of free choice; and skepticism, agnosticism, atheism, and hypocrisy seemed to be as typical of premodern society as they are of modern. The primary group was not destroyed by the industrial revolution; if anything, it is even more important now than it ever was in the past. There are more intense, intimate, informal relationships than there were in past times, and they are more psychologically meaningful if not more deeply binding than they used to be. Superstition has not vanished, as one need only read the daily astrology columns in the newspapers to know. The large corporate bureaucracy has indeed emerged as the characteristic institution of the modern world, but that does not mean that all the informal, intimate, personal loyalty relationships in the past have been wiped away. On the contrary, the affluence, the speed of transportation and communication that the corporate bureaucracies ensure have undoubtedly expanded the possibilities for primary group relationships. Nor is there any evidence at all that contemporary humankind has any less need to answer questions of ultimate meaning than did any of its predecessors. And the desperate quest for something to belong to manifested in the encounter, ESP, charismatic, Esalen, TM, and similar movements indicates that the autonomous, independent, rational, scientific individual still needs desperately to belong to a small, warm, supportive community.

Christopher Lasch has delivered a devastating indictment of the

TABLE 2

Modernization Model

As Description	As Norm To Be Rejected*
1. Modernization frees individual from ties and obligations imposed by accidents of birth, leading to personal autonomy and maturity and social and territorial mobility, e.g., ties of geography, ethnic group, religion, family of origin, occupational inheritance, political traditions, hereditary and sacral authority, and, more recently, sexual role definition.	1. Loss of support provided by old times—lonely crowd, one-dimensional man.
2. Family life marked by romantic love, emotional intimacy, nonauthoritarian socialization, and awareness of needs of children.	2. Trap of bourgeois marriage
3. Assumption by specific institutions (usually large, formal, and bureaucratic) of roles formerly played by undifferentiated family and church.	3. Role diffusion because of inconsistent demands.
4. Organization of institutions of "rational," "scientific," and bureaucratic principles instead of sacred or hereditary symbols.	4. Alienation, normlessness, rootlessness.
5. Interaction partners (economic, political, sexual, neighborhood, and so on) chosen on the basis of personal decision—presumed to be rational, individual, and career oriented.	5. Mass society, oppression of individual by "system."
6. Personality characterized by self-control, deferred gratification, independent decision making (identification with and internalization of Oedipal authority) as opposed to impulsive, emotional, dependent, labile personality (dependence on pre-Oedipal authority).	6. Inability to give self in trust, openness, intimacy.
7. As a result, notable decline in importance of intimate, personal, informal, nonrational, local, permanent, loyalty-based relationships—both to individuals and social systems.	7. Quest for community.

*Defenders of modernization often simultaneously depict it as a "description" (the way things have been and are) and a "norm" (the way they must be or ought to be). Critics generally accept it as a description but question it as a norm or an ideal. Some (like me) question its adequacy as a description.

modernization myth in his review article on the history of family literature in the *New York Review of Books.* He says, "It is hard to give up a picture of the family which suggests . . . that earlier generations were incapable of understanding things we now take for granted, that they seldom attained our heights of feeling; that love, sex and personal autonomy are our own inventions." He goes on to characterize the modernization model: "The modernization picture, then, leads us to approach world food problems with counterproductive assumptions and family history with demonstrably false expectations. And yet we are still profoundly reluctant to give it up and begin to actively search for an alternative model."

Increasingly, social critics are saying that one can have the insights of science and the production of technology without necessarily suffering a vast soulless, irresponsible corporate bureaucracy; that in many of the underdeveloped countries, for example, one could use science and technology to double or triple food production without bringing in huge machines. For technology does not mean the machine; it merely means applying scientific understanding to the way we do things—and we can do that with simple tools, improved seed, better fertilizer, and more sophisticated forms of cultivation. The industrial revolution, it turns out, did not make the giant corporation necessary—nor the soulless city, alienated man, the corporate bureaucracy. There was bound to be some increase in size of human institutions if only because of economy of scale and expanding populations; however neither necessarily meant General Motors, the New York metropolitan area, or the Department of Health, Education and Welfare. The emergence of all these corporate monsters is the result neither of science and technology nor the industrial revolution but rather of a sense, a conviction, an ideology, that larger is better, which, of course, is the fundamental assumption of the modernization model. All the old ties are to be rooted out because they are old-fashioned, superstitious, reactionary, particularistic; they are to be replaced by formal, rational, contractual, bureaucratic ties, because that is the efficient, scientific way of running human affairs. Larger Is Better.

E. F. Schumacher is a sophisticated economist and one of a number of social critics who propound that "Small Is Beautiful." But "Larger Is Better" is still deeply imbedded in the social thinking of our society's intelligentsia.

One of the curious things about the modernization model is that to a very considerable extent it is sociological in origin. The great sociological thinkers of the nineteenth century (Robert Nisbet describes them brilliantly in his *Sociological Tradition*) saw that the old feudal world was dying. Most of them—especially the greatest of them all, Tonnies and Weber—lamented the passing of the organic society and looked with apprehension on its replacement, the bureaucratic society. But they thought change was inevitable and had to be accepted. However, paradoxically enough, most contemporary sociological research does not provide much support for the model. Many sophisticated sociologists reject it; thus one sociologist remarked to me, "Isn't it ironic that the historical demographers, who are collecting rich and fascinating data about the way people really lived three hundred years ago, are trying to fit their data into a model which they borrowed from us and which we have never bothered to prove at all?"

The rediscovery of the primary group—informal, intimate, person-oriented relationships—by the sociologists of the 1950s and 1960s, the rediscovery of ethnicity and superstition in the 1960s and 1970s, and the research hints of the prevalence of religious experience in the 1970s have all brought into serious question the *terminus ad quem* of the modernization model; and the historians of the family and the historical demographers have pretty well knocked the props out from under many of the assumptions of the *terminus a quo* of the model. Ironically, the family and demographic historians, who have done more to destroy the model than any other contemporary scholars, still ritualistically cite it.

Life has changed; we do not live the way our ancestors did. But most of the change can be adequately accounted for by better science, improved technology, superior transportation and communication, much better health care, greater abundance, and longer and more comfortable lives. None of these changes either requires or necessarily causes basic and fundamental changes in either human nature or the nature of human relationships. Society may be a good deal more complex, things may happen much more rapidly, we may be much more sophisticated in our understanding, and much more articulate and nuanced in our teminology. But we still have to die, we still eat, we still want to love, we still reproduce, we still wonder about the meaning of life, we still have to work, we still suffer loneliness, anxiety, and fear, we still band together with our family, our friends, those who think like us and with whom we are comfortable—our kind of people. The fundamental flaw in the modernization argument is to assume that more knowledge and greater skills and more conveniences and longer life fundamentally modifies the structure of human needs, human longings, human propensities. Such an assumption is always just that—an assumption that is beyond proof. A classic example of such an assumption is Alvin Toffler's book *Future Shock*. It piles up evidence about the pervasiveness and speed of change but consistently begs the question of whether change in the physical environment of humankind leads to any fundamental change in human personality. Toffler takes it for granted that there is such a connection; most people do. But it has never been proved, and so far as there is evidence, much of it runs in the contrary direction.

The modernization model is flattering, for it means that we are basically different from and superior to our predecessors. They were ignorant, unenlightened, superstitious; we are progressive, enlightened, rational, scientific. We are the wave of history, the leading edge of progress; we are superior to our predecessors and are pointing the direction for the future, which will be even better than our present. An ultimate absurdity is reached in Margaret Mead's notion that the young people of the 1960s were truly a different brand of human, because unlike their grandparents, who had roots in the past, or their parents, who lived in the present, the children of the 1960s had their roots in the future. It sounds great, but when you stop to think about what it means, you realize it means nothing.

In addition to being flattering, modernization is also reassuring. We are assured that things will get better and whatever problems we have represent temporary setbacks in the admirable forward march of history. Of course modernization does fit some of the evidence, because things have changed, after all; but there is no evidence that the basic structures of human relationships have changed in the slightest, and there is substantial evidence that if one pushes the implications of the modernization model far enough, the result is not improvement but disaster. (Look at New York City, for example.)

Let me cite an example from research done on Iowa families in the early part of this century.* There was a major educational conflict in the public school systems of Iowa at the turn of the century between the self-proclaimed "modernizers" and the "traditionalists," the former being for the most part Yankees led by educators trained at the University of Chicago and the latter being German Lutheran and German Catholic farmers (turn-of-the-century ethnics, in other words). The modernizers were in favor of school consolidation as a prelude to educational achievement. One got ahead in society, they argued, with profound American faith, by being educated; and you really couldn't get a good education in the small, two-, four-, six-room classroom schools of the rural school district. Therefore, to improve education and hence occupational achievement, one had to eliminate the small school districts and combine them into large, consolidated grammar schools and high schools.

The traditionalists argued vigorously that they wanted to control the schools their children went to, and that local control of school systems was the most democratic way. They were also profoundly skeptical about the advantages of education, especially since they were making at least as much money, if not more, on their farms than were the Yankee modernizers on theirs.

Well, as one might suspect, the modernizers won. The local schools

*Richard Jensen, "Education and the Modernization of the Midwest" (mimeographed report). Chicago: Newberry Library.

were abolished, consolidated school districts were delineated, large schools constructed, and most of the Yankees, armed with their college degrees, departed for the city, leaving the traditionalists to man the farms in Iowa and feed a substantial proportion of the human race. Another victory for progress.

Only now it would appear that school decentralization and local control is the wave of the future. Indeed, all over the country, school consolidation and centralization had barely won the day when the cry for school decentralization began to be heard. And there is no particular evidence that what happens in the schools makes much of a contribution to life success—at least not when compared to what goes on at home. Indeed, a good deal of the correlation between education and occupation simply results from the fact that educational requirements have been imposed for many occupations in the naive belief that what happens in school affects one's ability to carry on in the occupational world. However, the correlation between education and income is very moderate to say the least, and black Americans, after twenty years of pushing educational opportunity, are now beginning to think that they may have made a mistake, and that education doesn't lead to income so much as income leads to more education and then to higher levels of income. Ivan Illich, the famous radical theorist, is calling now for the "deschooling" of society, which puts him in the same camp as the German Lutheran and German Catholic traditionalists in Iowa at the turn of the century.

Big schools are not better schools, modernized education is not necessarily better than traditional education. Big modern schools do not necessarily prepare one for either life or occupational success; the family and family values were and are and probably always will be much more important than what goes on in the schools.

Immense efforts have been expended on "modernizing" those groups which have resisted modernization—German farmers, Polish and Italian immigrants, black poor—on the grounds that once they were modernized, undisorganized, unalienated, they would become good, hard-working, achieving Americans like everyone else. Now it appears that just the opposite was the case: occupational and economic success comes to ordinary people within a minority group not by alienating them from their past but by reinforcing their sense of cultural and personal identity—especially by providing them with enough income with which to have a decent life. They didn't need modernization, it turned out; all they needed was money.

One of my colleagues once asked me whether there were ever any cases of money being provided to disadvantaged poor with the result that they began to acquire middle-class values and middle-class life styles. I asked him what the hell he thought had been the story of the Irish, the Italians, and the Polish immigrants. They were given money (which they earned, of course) and they began to live like very respectable middle-class Americans, which they always wanted to be in the first place. In the process, they held onto their religion, their families, their neighborhood loyalties, and many of the other things which they brought from the old world and which, after all, turned out not to be obstacles to either economic success or social respectability.

Professor Donald Campbell, in his presidential address to the American Psychological Association in 1975, argued to the validity of ancient religious symbol systems and moral codes. Original sin, moral values, and religious symbols, he stated, were the result of a social revolution which has checked the human aggressiveness that developed through biological evolution. Abandoning all these things, Campbell suggested, was not progress but regression. What one needs in the world today, he said, is not fewer inhibitions but perhaps more, not more spontaneity and self-expression but more altruism.

One might quibble with Campbell about whether there really has been a "biological evolution" of human aggressiveness; one also might quibble as to whether altruism is not, after all, the highest form of human self-expression (though heaven knows most psychologists would deny that). But those are minor points. Campbell has stood the modernization model on its head, and he calls for at least a reappraisal of the values of the past if not a return to them.

There is no surer way in the world to be called a "conservative."

And if you are a psychologist, to be a conservative is the kiss of death; for if progress is good and stasis is bad, discontinuity virtuous and continuity evil, if the old is always wrong and the new is always right, if the modern is always better and the traditional worse, if breaking something up is always liberal and protecting it always conservative, then anyone who thinks there might be anything in the past that is superior to the present is both a conservative and bad. All one needs to do in many intellectual circles is to refer to one's opponent as a conservative or a traditionalist and two-thirds of the battle is won. Modernization is not only the wave of the future, it is liberal, enlightened, and moral; to stand against it is to reveal oneself as conservative, unenlightened, and morally weak. Mind you, these are not points to be argued. As Campbell himself wryly points out, "As soon as one of his critics could establish that Campbell was talking about something that might be called 'original sin,' the critic withdrew from the field in triumph, claiming victory." The issue is not whether there may be something in reality that corresponds to the old image of original sin; the issue is merely whether you can convict your opponent of using the concept of original sin. Do that and you have won the day.

So even though social critics doubt that modernization has turned out to be all that good a thing, and even though social researchers find vast amounts of data that do not seem to fit either the beginning or the end of the modernization image, and even though radical social critics (as well as reductionist psychologists like Campbell) are calling for dramatically new approaches to our thinking about society, the modernization model still dominates the thinking of most Americans, particularly in the intellectual and cultural elites—as do the secularization model of religion and the melting pot model of pluralism, for neither one of which is there any more "proof" than there is for modernization.

The indictment against neighborhoods, then, is simply that they are "antimodern." They are a regression to more primitive and premodern ways of living. The neighborhood asserts the importance of the primordial, the local, the geographic, the familial against the demands of the bureaucratized, rationalized, scientific, corporate society. The neighborhood is a relic of the premodern, reactionary, feudal, and superstitious past. One may have pleasant memories of one's own neighborhood and nostalgically lament its passing, one may shake one's head in reflective dismay at a society without communities as warm and as close as the old neighborhoods were; but it's a price that has to be paid for human progress.

It does little good to argue that such concepts as "necessary price," "inevitable progress," "march of history," and "modern man" are mostly verbal and intellectual constructs without any reality in the world beyond the human mind. But that is precisely why they are so important to those who are alienated from their own pasts, their own heritages, their own neighborhoods, their own kind. And it is one of those alienated isolates who will raise the question at the end of the lecture, "But don't you really think that neighborhoods are less important than they used to be?" Or, "Don't you really think that ethnicity is vanishing in American society?" Or, "Don't you think people aren't as religious as they used to be?"

What the hell do you say to someone like that? After you have spent the whole evening trotting out evidence that small, local communities are as important to people today as they ever were, that questions of the meaning of human life are as important as they ever were, and that the desire to pass on one's values and heritage to one's children is at least as powerful as it ever was, and somebody persists in asking such questions, you cannot say a thing to them, because they won't hear you.

The neighborhood is rejected by our intellectual and cultural elites (save for a growing number of both radical and conservative critics) precisely because the neighborhood is not modern, and what is not modern is conservative, reactionary, unprogressive, unenlightened, superstitious, and just plain wrong. You may tolerate neighborhoods, you may even acknowledge that they occasionally do some good things; but for the love of heaven you don't want people "celebrating" them.

Neighborhoods are narrow, they are local, they are "parochial." How can any well-educated, sophisticated, cosmopolitan, "modern" person possibly believe that there is anything good from something as parochial as the neighborhood?

How indeed.

7

The Case
for the Neighborhood

Neighborhoods are for kids especially
. . . because kids are alive to its wonder and magic . . .
the slide . . . the football game . . . the birthday party . . .
the ride in an old station wagon . . .
neighborhoods are for kids of any age . . .
and some of us stay kids all our lives, thank God. . . .

It seems to me that the ultimate issue about the neighborhood is philosophical or even theological. One can easily score points about the economic reasons for sustaining and protecting neighborhood viability, but people who view neighborhoods as reactionary, primitive, particularistic communities are willing to bear the economic costs of grinding them into rubble (although, truth to say, it is usually someone else who bears the cost) in order to rid the environment of such an archaic remnant of a long-gone (they hope) and inferior society.

My own philosophical assumption is that we are social animals, and both the words "social" and "animal" are important. We have physical bodies like all the other animals, and we must cooperate with one another to stay alive, to reproduce, and to bring our offspring into adulthood. Of course we are social animals. Yet the modernization ideology, which I described in the previous chapter, calls into serious question, implicitly at any rate, both the social and the animal nature of humankind. It sees us, first of all, breaking away from the rootedness, the ties, the boundaries, the limitations, the constraints that are imposed on us by biology, physiology, and geography. The liberating effects of the Reformation, the Renaissance, the scientific, technical, and intellectual revolutions were to produce men and women who were not tied to place, family, tradition, tribe, heritage; they could move anywhere in the world and with any group of people from purely rational, autonomous, independent, universalistic values and motives. But such creatures would be archangels.

The physiology of our bodies reacts vigorously even against jet travel and demands to be given time to catch up. The body, apparently, is prepared to accept the change of one time zone a day (about the pace of a transatlantic steamship) and little more. We move from place to place very quickly now, but we pay a price. Furthermore, the human personality seems predisposed to established routines, physical and temporal "Indian paths," which free us from the necessity of making decisions every day about how to go to work, what time to get up, what to do next. Without these routine habits we would spend so much time making decisions over commonplace events that we would have little time or psychic energy left for anything else. The body and the personality (which is structured by the body, of course) seem to operate according to preestablished rhythms—the body necessarily, the personality whenever it can. These psychological and physiological rhythms involve stability and familiarity of place. It seems that geographical familiarity is also psychologically reassuring. We are less afraid and have less need to respond aggressively when we are on familiar ground, or when we are relating to others with whom we have established certain relational paradigms. From the purely physiological viewpoint, for example, sex with one partner is no different than sex with another partner; in both cases there is tension release. However, human sexuality is not merely physiological but a complex of the physical and the psychological; and there is solid evidence for thinking that the physiological payoff in sex is much richer when the act takes place with someone who shares a pattern and a context with us. Finally, while childrearing can be carried on by any adult, and while there probably isn't anything in humans that corresponds to the "maternal instinct" of mammals, there is still a strong predisposition to establish a psychic bond with a child whose existence we are physiologically and biologically responsible for. And that bond is usually a reciprocal one which extends to the cultural heritage the child has acquired from us.

To put the matter differently, if the human animal did not need sleep, rest, routine, familiarity, parents, and a mate, then he might surely be the autonomous universalistic creature the modernization theory would make him; but in fact his very corporeal nature inclines him to an existence in which he has certain physiological and biological roots. He tends to be part of a given family, to live in a given place, to set biological and physiological rhythms, and to form affiliations which resonate with the place and its people. Humankind establishes a special relationship with place because it is a bodily creature, possessed of bodily rhythms and needing certain bodily relationships, which, usually at any rate, occur in the physical space in which the human animal has to be. The neighborhood simply is one of the places in the contemporary world where humans live and where they experience and organize the physiological and psychological rhythms of their lives, rhythms which become deeply involved with that physical place.

People can go elsewhere, of course; they can leave their place, but they usually "pull up roots" reluctantly. It means reorganizing the paths, the traces, the patterns, the rhythms of life. Humans can do it, of course, and it is probably easier for them to do it now than it was in the past when "to move away" mean to sever old ties forever. I can fly to County Mayo, for example, and when I get over the jet lag, the trip will undoubtedly have been less costly to me in terms of my physical resources than when my grandparents journeyed from there to County Cook. And should I decide to settle in County Mayo, it would surely be less frightening and less disruptive for me than it was for my grandparents to accustom themselves to the New World. Yet I would find it at least as hard, I think, to adjust to the pace and style of life there as they did when they first came to Chicago. More importantly, perhaps, I doubt that it would be much easier for me to break the network of relationships in which I presently live than it was for them to break theirs. It is always hard to say goodbye.

And to say goodbye is to emphasize the social nature of humankind. There is no possibility of separating the animal nature of humankind from its social nature. That which is social about us is rooted in our animality, which is in its turn inevitably social. Indeed, humankind, as the anthropologist Clifford Geertz points out, was social long before it became human; it was the social nature of the prehominids that enabled them to evolve into higher forms of life. No culture without man, says Geertz, but also no man without culture. We need other human beings to come into the world, to keep us alive during childhood, to care for us when we are sick and old, to bury us when we die, to form families with us, to help us defend ourselves from danger, to find food, raise our crops, build our homes, teach us to walk, to talk, to pray, and to love. We have strong tendencies toward egoism and selfishness, aggressiveness and destructiveness; but we also need other human beings, and we know that we need them. We are afraid of risking ourselves with others; but biologically and physiologically we have no choice. When we take the risk of trusting someone else, we find that it is both a scary and a pleasant experience. One of the reasons we know that some of our early predecessors were human is that we can tell from their grave sites that they protected and provided for some members of the tribe who were physically maimed and unable to take care of themselves. There is a jungle tendency, no doubt, in a human personality, but there is also a strong cooperative tendency. We may hurt one another, but we cannot get along without one another. One may not choose to call this basic conflict "original sin," but whatever we call it, no one who has ever lived with human beings for very long or who reads the daily newspapers can be in much doubt about the existence of the flaw.

Those who believe in the modernization model are well aware of this flaw and are usually prepared to acknowledge that autonomous, deracinated, alienated "modern man" is a highly aggressive, selfish individual; he is Hobbes's "jungle savage" released from the constraints of his tribe. If a modernizer leans in the capitalist direction, he believes that this fundamental selfishness of autonomous modern man is good because, through some marvelous alchemy, individual selfishness—within the restraints of enlightened self-interest—leads to the common welfare. If he is a liberal or a socialist, the modernizer would be inclined to argue that the selfishness and aggressiveness is not part of human nature but is rather the result of the oppression of social or psychological structures, and that if one changes the structure of society and of human relationships, man's natural cooperative and loving characteristics will emerge (usually in a socialist or quasisocialist welfare state). If one is a social biologist or an ethologist, the modernist would not deny, as do the liberals and socialists, the fundamental destructiveness and aggressiveness of the human personality but argue that knowledge and understanding, or, if one's proclivities are behaviorist, proper conditioning would restrain and correct if not eliminate them.

From the point of view of Catholic social theory (as well, it would seem to me, from the point of view of common sense), all such theories and arguments about the selfish and aggressive nature of human nature overlook the strong basic cooperative tendencies of the human personality. Human beings tend to form dense, intimate, "organic" relationship networks in which stable, supportive, frequently affectionate and often profoundly loyal interactions emerge. There may be conflict and competition in these relationships—for even in the strongest love there is still room for conflict and competition—but most of the time these relationships are more cooperative than competitive. While there are some human beings who can live without such relationships for a time at least, and while there are others who are so psychically maimed that they cannot trust themselves to any other human beings (we call them psychopaths), the ordinary, typical human proclivity is to establish relationships of at least some trust and affection with many if not most of those with whom one interacts frequently and routinely. Such relationships are not without ambivalence or suspicion, for the basic human flaw is fear or, more specifically, distrust, which is self-conscious fear. Distrust is inevitable in any creature which is not only mortal but self-consciously so. Human relationships become healthy and wholesome not when you remake human nature but when you provide humans with the structures and the motivations for overcoming their distrust sufficiently to give themselves in affectionate vulnerability one to another.

But affection and vulnerability imply familiarity, which does not, contrary to the popular saying, breed contempt; rather it breeds intimacy and results from intimacy. We tend to become intimate with those who are familiar, and we are familiar indeed with those with whom we become intimate. Contempt enters the picture only when we find ourselves threatened by the vulnerability of intimacy.

Or to put the matter at its most simple and elemental, one can hardly imagine a situation in which two very attractive members of the opposite sex, apparently unattached, ride up and down in an elevator every day for several months and give absolutely no sign that they are aware of the existence of one another. No, they will begin to smile at each other, then chat pleasantly about the weather, begin to exchange information about themselves outside the elevator, and then perhaps meet for lunch or a drink after work. At that point they may begin to date, which can lead to nothing or everything. But given the nature of human nature it is highly improbable that they will ignore one another in their frequent encounters on the elevator.

When we live, work, and cross paths with others frequently we tend to become friendly with them or to fight with them—and in many cases we do both. However universalistic the world may be, most people end up marrying those who live near them or who work with them. Social, structural, or cultural factors may modify the propensity to psychic familiarity with those with whom we are physically familiar. The Protestants and Catholics of Northern Ireland, for example, may be physically juxtaposed yet be very unlikely to become close friends—though frequently that happens too, despite the centuries of religious conflict between them. One may also be suspicious of the local policemen, particularly if they are racially different; and one may have strong animosity for certain neighbors because of previous conflicts, competitions, or misunderstandings. But when all of these phenomena are acknowledged, it still must be said that it is very hard not to smile at someone you see every day. It would very surprising if frequent interaction patterns did not normally lead to at least courteous acknowledgment of the other's presence if not to friendship.

Human beings, in other words, both physically and psychologically, are predisposed to informal, intimate, affectionate, trusting relationships with those with whom they share the same place. There are various factors which may interfere with such relationships coming into being or which may inhibit their growth or even destroy them; but the propensity is still there. There is no evidence at all that the social, economic, industrial, transportation, communication, and life-cycle changes of the last several hundred years have modified that propensity one bit. All the evidence we know from empirical sociology and psychology suggests that the model of the nature of human nature on which the modernizers operate simply doesn't correspond with the way humankind really is. Increasingly, some of the better social scientists are beginning to acknowledge that.

Our life takes place in a physical and social context. We may move from one context to another, but the image of the isolated, alienated, lonely individual, cut off from all human relationships, save perhaps for that with his current sexual partner, is a fantasy of mass-society social theorists and future-shock pop sociologists. It has absolutely nothing to do with the way most people have lived most of the time throughout the whole of human history. Indeed it is precisely those modernizers who most vigorously and enthusiastically denounce the neighborhood who are also the most likely to spend most of their time—occupational, recreational, and sexual—with people who do exactly the same kind of work, share exactly the same kind of values, and probably live almost the same place they do. It is all right, in other words, for *them* to have neighborhoods but not the rest of us.

Still more must be said if one is looking at society through the perspective of Catholic or communal social theory. The dignity of the individual human person depends ultimately on his freedom and his inviolability. We are only free and inviolable when we are masters of our own destiny; we come together in human society because we are constrained to by our biological and psychological natures but also so that through mutual cooperation we can grow to fuller, richer, and more authentic human beings. Society exists to facilitate the growth and development of the individual person, and the state is nothing more than that institution which the persons in the society establish in order to facilitate and promote the general welfare—but only to the extent that the individual persons have delegated power and authority to the state. Society does not arise out of contract; it is given wherever there are two or more humans. But the state does come from contract; the authority of the government depends upon the consent of the governed, and governance without consent, whether it be in Cuba, Poland, the Soviet Union, China, Tanzania, Sweden, England, or even in some of the oppressive situations in which government power has become all encompassing in the United States, becomes tyranny. Authority without consent is slavery.

But the dignity and the freedom of the individual person, dependent as it is on the extent to which he controls his own life, can only exist when as much social and political power as possible is maintained at the lowest possible level in the society. The dictum "small is beautiful" may be a bit too romantic for Catholic social theory, but the Catholic principle of subsidiarity or subsidiary function can be articulated in the somewhat less poetic but more precise slogan, "no bigger than necessary." Nothing should be done by a higher or larger organization that can be done as well by a lower and smaller one. Nothing should be done by the international community that can be done by the state, nothing by the state that can be done as well by the city, nothing by the city that can be done by the neighborhood, nothing by the neighborhood that can be done by the family. Ultimately, this is the only efficient way to run a society, since it is the only way that makes the most use of individual talents and capabilities and also the only way that most effectively guarantees the intelligent and committed cooperation of citizens in the decisions society reaches. But quite apart from, or perhaps antecedent to, decisions about efficiency, the principle of subsidiarity must be honored because it is the only way one can protect, promote, and defend the freedom, the dignity, the authenticity of the individual human person. It is also the only way one can best facilitate the individual's growth in intimate vulnerability in a dense organic network of relationships which constitute the matrix of his life.

The modernizers who do not believe in this matrix or believe that it is reactionary may argue that "bigger is better." They want to abolish the function of the neighborhood; indeed they appear to want to turn the running of the human race into some kind of huge civil service, presided over by the juvenile delinquents at the United Nations. They may even get away with it. But such an oppressive world bureaucracy will discover that out in the neighborhoods, the villages, the desert oases, the rural crossroads, and the jungle settlements there will always be restless, determined individuals who will not knuckle under and who will demand and take freedom over their own lives—even if it means sabotaging the neatly organized bureaucracy. You can, in other words, ignore neighborhoods, destroy them, and obliterate them; but beware, they will spring up somewhere else. As long as you have humans who are social animals, necessarily driven by both their social and animal nature into intimate vulnerability in which they search for freedom and love—frequently mistakenly, often desperately, but always persistently —you will have neighborhoods.

Because that's what the neighborhood is all about—freedom and love.

Many neighborhoods may have been low on both, but that's a failure of the ideal to be actualized in practice. If you abolish the neighborhood or its functional equivalent in favor of a homogenized and bureaucratized society, you will have neither freedom nor love; you are very likely to have opposition, sabotage, and eventually even revolt.

The neighborhood, then, as a strong, powerful unit of urban society, is a postulate of the principle of subsidiary function; if you believe in "no bigger than necessary" you have got to believe in the neighborhood. Or, to put the matter somewhat differently, if you believe that human nature is the nature of a social animal, you have got to believe in the neighborhood. The modernizers believe in neither, and it is therefore virtually impossible to argue with them. For them human nature in its present form is both more autonomous and less cooperative, and subsidiarity is a reactionary reduction of a social philosophy that believes in the dignity of the individual person, and that society exists for the person instead of vice versa. In the final analysis the conflict over neighborhoods is a conflict over the nature and dignity of the individual. The modernizers do not believe that it is a good thing to trust the individual with that much freedom.

If one believes in "no bigger than necessary" and therefore supports neighborhoods, one automatically guarantees a highly variegated and pluralistic city. If the individual human person is given the greatest amount of freedom to develop his own unique and special talents, and if the dense organic, informal, intimate interaction networks in which he lives and loves are given their greatest possible freedom, they too will develop that which is most unique and special in them. Under such circumstances variegated and diversified interaction networks are bound to emerge. For those who like their cities neat, orderly, and "rational," this will be an affront. Better a carefully planned checkerboard, interlaced with straight expressways out of which spring long, orderly, stately rows of high-rise apartment buildings than the crazy quilt patchwork variety of the city where there is a maximum emphasis on individual and neighborhood independence and creativity. Better the New York of Robert Moses than the Chicago of Richard Daley.

Like hell, say I.

If you want a neat, uniform, blueprint-designed city, then turn it over to the modernizers, the city planners, the scientists, the rationalists, the people who thought up high-rise public housing. If you want a rich, variegated, exciting, diversified, stimulating, vital city, then turn it back to the neighborhoods and give them the maximum possible amount of freedom. To put the matter differently, if you want a city for humans, maximize neighborhood; if you want a city for planners, bureaucrats, and professors, destroy them.

The issue is ultimately a philosophical one, as I said in the beginning of this chapter. The modernization model is the enemy of the neighborhood; it grows out of a philosophy of the nature of human nature which sees humankind as both able to evolve away from local, geographic, "nonrational" intimacies and in the process of doing so. Support for the neighborhood as a matter of philosophical principle comes from a different view of human nature, one which believes that humankind is able to transcend the limitations of time and place but is also inevitably rooted in its own particular piece of ground. About such philosophical differences there cannot be any ultimate resolution, I think. The modernist says that the good life will only really come when we have completely left behind our narrow, particularistic localism; the other says that the good life, or at least the best kind of life we can have in this vale of tears, will only come when there is a maximum amount of freedom and independence at the lowest possible social level. Whatever the social theorists may say, the overwhelming burden of the weight of empirical evidence supports the neighborhood position. With some exceptions, humankind, as we know it up to and including the present, has been local. Even the highly mobile citizens of the transient society sink shallow roots in whatever new place they may find themselves in order to establish the rhythms of social life necessary for the normal human personality. That they dare not sink roots deeply in commitment, affiliation, and affection is only to prevent pain when they move on. That we may eventually evolve a species of humankind that does not need roots is an interesting speculation, but one for which there is very little in the way of empirical confirmation despite desperate attempts to find it.

And I think there is no doubt which of the two visions appealed to the men who founded our republic. Perhaps the most profound contribution to the history of political theory, developed by Wilson of Pennsylvania at the Constitutional Convention, was the notion of limited sovereignty: all those powers which were not specifically delegated by the Constitution to the federal government were inherent to the states or to the individuals who constituted the society. This is subsidiarity with a vengeance.

James Madison believed in neighborhoods.

8

Support for
Your Local Neighborhood

Hamburgers . . . milk shakes . . . the S and L . . .
the boys' club . . . the local movie . . . the neighborhood bakery . . .
the ward organization office . . . all can be saved and renewed . . .
only the romantic pessimist despairs of the resiliency
of neighborhoods. . . .

If neighborhoods are so "natural," and if they are so essential to a human and humane urban life, why do they collapse so quickly? I have argued in this book that they collapse because those who think about, plan for, and administer the complexities of urban life do not believe in neighborhoods and think that they are reactionary and an obstacle to progress. Therefore, those who are responsible for the establishment of programs and the enforcement of laws either actively attack neighborhoods or passively tolerate practices, policies, and processes which lead to neighborhood deterioration and decay. In some instances laws are not enforced, in others laws are not passed, and in still other instances, practices are tolerated which are patently unwise on the grounds that it is not worth making a major effort to stop them.

I do not propose to write a technical monograph of neighborhood problems or a practical handbook on how to respond to these problems*; but it is essential to my passionate plea for neighborhoods that I sketch out the problems and indicate directions of some of the more obvious solutions—even though such solutions will only begin to be applied when neighborhood people themselves are powerful enough and determined enough to force them on a reluctant body of thinkers, planners, programmers, and administrators.

1. *Housing stock.* Most urban slums were eliminated from American life in the decades immediately after the Second World War. By "slums" I mean that housing which was structurally inferior or so old as to be unusable or so poorly made as to be unfit for human habitation. Those buildings which are considered urban slums today are mostly buildings which are not structurally inferior and either are or can be readily made fit for comfortable, dignified human habitation. They have become slums either through neglect or through conscious policy, and since it is easier if not cheaper to build new suburban housing than

---

*The best sources for detailed information on neighborhood revitalization are the National Center for Urban Ethnic Affairs, 1521 16th St., N.W., Washington D.C., and the National Training and Information Center, 121 West Superior St., Chicago, Illinois. The Washington Center's "Bibliography on Neighborhood Reinvestment" is a particularly useful technical document.

to rehabilitate old urban housing, the principal dynamics at work in the American housing market push toward the deterioration of perfectly good urban housing stock. Indeed, so rapid is the deterioration of structurally solid and humanly habitable buildings that housing stock can easily be considered "old" only fifteen years after it has been built.

Yet government housing policies, particularly government mortgage policies which subsidize the upper-middle-class, single-family home purchased by the well-to-do through tax exemptions for mortgage interest payments, actively encourage the deterioration and the forced obsolescence of homes which are at least as good as and often much better than the new housing units that are replacing them in the hinterlands of the big cities. In July of 1975, President Ford (which is to say his ghost writers) submitted to Congress the seventh annual housing report, a document which is substantially less than honest in facing the fact that federal policies are contributing substantially to the deterioration of the existing stock of habitable homes. Lip service is paid to the proposition that the existing housing stock "is a precious resource which should not be wasted or callously disregarded," and adds that "in an economy of growing scarcity, a prudent policy will seek to avert such losses through halting deterioration and restoring usefulness by correction of deficiencies and upgrading to current standards for housing services." The housing report blandly admits, however, that "rehabilitation of deteriorated older structures in marginal neighborhoods has proven to be a most difficult program to administer."

It is a "most difficult program to administer" because neither the laws nor the policies nor the procedures of the Department of Housing and Urban Development take seriously rehabilitation of neighborhoods. All the vested interests, bureaucratic, financial, commercial, and political, are oriented toward the endless construction of new suburbs. Urban neighborhoods do not have the power, the clout, or the money to resist the process—at least they have not had it so far. Such organizations as Chicago's Metropolitan Area Housing Alliance (MAHA), which is multireligious, multiethnic, and multiracial, are beginning to build a solid power base, but with the exception of the few organizations like MAHA, neighborhood people have a hard time getting existing HUD regulations and federal laws enforced for the rehabilitation of existing housing, much less getting new laws passed to strengthen rehabilitation programs.

Quite simply, among the biggest weaknesses of middle-aged housing is the deterioration of plumbing, the absence of heat-saving insulation (including thermopane or storm windows), and inadequate electric circuits to bear the load of the tremendous increase of power usage by such now-indispensable gadgets as televisions, dishwashers, automatic dryers, and air conditioners. Many pre–World War I homes and apartments are far more gracious and well built than anything being constructed in the new mass-produced suburbs, but the plumbing, the electricity, insulation, and windows of these old buildings are simply not up to the standards middle-class Americans expect—even lower-middle-class Americans. Particularly their kitchens are the sort that the modern American woman (to say nothing of her gourmet-cooking husband) simply will refuse to work in if she possibly can. It is much cheaper and a much wiser use of resources, of course, to modernize the middle-aged or even the old house than to build a new one. Strangely enough, however, few of our ecological and environmental enthusiasts seem to think that the planned deterioration of urban neighborhoods is a form of environmental waste.

2. *The dual housing market.* In many cities there are really two housing markets, one for blacks and one for whites. If you are black, you have to pay more for a home, because there is a smaller supply of homes available for blacks than for whites. The laws of supply and demand being what they are, if the supply is small while demand is fixed, the price is high. The dual housing market is maintained by real estate companies sometimes in a sincere effort to preserve the neighborhood from the apparently inevitable consequences of racial change but also because for many real estate companies—particularly the fly-by-night, fast-buck, wheeler-dealer type —the dual housing market is a source of immense profits. The absence of effective antidiscrimination measures in the real estate

market enables some real estate companies to exploit racial preju-
dice and racial fear and to make vast sums of money in the process.
The justification heard from such operators is that if they don't
make it, someone else will.

It is not clear whether there are any really effective ways to enforce
antidiscriminatory practices in the housing market, particularly in the
suburban areas where the white upper middle class effectively conspires
through zoning regulations, implicit real estate practices, and the legal
fiction of city boundaries to keep city problems and city problem people
out of their preserves. My own personal conviction is that only when
the federal government is willing to use its very considerable housing
resources and power to vigorously reinforce voluntary metropolitan
integration will we be able to expect the dual metropolitan housing
market to go away. Thus it should be very simple, for example, to
require that before a homeowner can deduct the interest payment on
his house from his federal income tax return that his residential suburb
will have to prove that within its boundaries are, let us say, half the
proportion of nonwhite minorities to be found in the metropolitan
area. In a metropolitan area like Chicago, this would mean that each
one of the suburbs would have to show a 5 per cent segment of its
population is nonwhite—a trivial proportion in any one suburb, but
when multiplied by the all the suburbs in Cook, Lake, and DuPage
counties, it could mean salvation for the city. Such a requirement
would readily eliminate all problems about busing school children and
would be far more easy to enforce than court-ordered school integration
programs. I never could figure out why the militant white and black
organizations such as the NAACP do not put their energies into getting such federal legislation instead of harassing poor whites in the
inner city who are not their real enemies to begin with. Obviously,
many white suburbanites who have fled the city to escape its problems
would vigorously oppose such legislation. I suspect that many judges,
so eager to move the children of the urban poor and urban middle class
around the city in school buses, would quickly rule such a provision
unconstitutional. Still, when the alternative is an all-black city

and all-white suburbs, one might consider the value of a constitutional amendment.

The tax incentive method could also be used very effectively to reinforce the rehabilitation of old structures as an alternative to the construction of new ones. Thus while the interest on loans for the construction of new homes or the purchase of new homes might rate a tax *deduction* (if a suburb or neighborhood had its quota of non-whites), a tax *credit* might be given for interest on loans to rehabilitate existing structures. The difference between a tax deduction and a tax credit, as most Americans know, is that the credit is subtracted from the tax bill, the deduction only from gross income. Such tax credits (a common enough subsidy in other areas of American life) might enable a lending institution to charge higher interest rates on rehabilitation jobs and thus make such loans more attractive to the institution, while at the same time these loans would still be less expensive for the borrower, because of the tax credit, than the loan to purchase another home or to build a new one.

3. *Panic peddling.* The most vicious of all the urban crooks are those real estate operators who deliberately and consciously profit from the tension of racial change by stirring up panic in neighborhoods threatened with it. They have gone so far as to hire black teenagers to wander through a neighborhood to create fear. Such panic peddlers are also called "blockbusters" because once they sell a home to a black family they quickly move in on other homeowners to panic them with threats and warnings, and then proceed to buy up their homes cheaply, selling them to more black families at inflated prices. Many cities have ordinances against panic peddlers, but they are weak and difficult to enforce, and the penalties are usually small fines, which make little dents in the blockbuster's profits. Occasionally a real estate license is revoked, but the blockbusting company quickly reappears under another name. Only jail sentences are likely to deter such pirates; urban governments are loathe to impose severe penalties, especially since panic peddlers are often generous campaign and party contributors.

There are a number of neat tricks that can be pulled to make money in a racially changing neighborhood. Panic causes the value of homes to decline rapidly. Real estate companies, perhaps profiting from the panic, perhaps causing it, buy up large numbers of homes at much less than their realistic value. Then the homes are appraised—often by dubious techniques—at much higher values and sold on FHA-guaranteed mortgage loans to minority group members. The money is usually provided not by a bank or by a savings and loan association but by a "mortgage company" which specializes in FHA-guaranteed loans. (These companies are often owned by out-of-town banks, since you don't get into shady business in your own city. New York banks, for example, own mortgage companies in Chicago.) The payments are often too high for those who have the loans; often within a year or two the housebuyer defaults and the company collects a tidy profit from the FHA. The house may be sold again, or more likely it will be already in a state of decay and will be abandoned, to be turned over to the city in lieu of taxes and torn down. Ironically, the "progressive" 1968 Housing Act makes such practices possible. The good intentions of liberal lawmakers once again led to a decline of housing stock and urban neighborhoods.* The regulations on depreciation of multidwelling housing units are such that once a building begins to decay, it is much cheaper to tear it down and build a new one than it is to rehabilitate it. (The city will tear it down for you and sell you the cleared property cheap. But by that time, of course, the neighborhood will have been long gone.)

There is an effective and simple way to beat the panic peddlers: property value insurance. Much of the panic in a racially changing neighborhood is financial. It does no good for sociologists to produce research evidence that demonstrates property values eventually go up in a racially changing neighborhood. Given the dual real estate market,

---

*It is generally agreed that the best legislation on income and investment disclosure —in effect, antiredlining—is the Chicago ordinance. Community organizers assert that it is far more progressive than the existing federal legislation (which forces lending institutions to reveal only where they make their loans, not where they get their deposits) and state laws.

of course they do. But in the short run, when blacks are moving into an area and whites are moving out, property values plummet, and life savings put into a home can easily be slashed. Hundreds of thousands of people have taken severe financial drubbings by trying to stay in a racially changing neighborhood. It is not those who get out quickly who lose money but those who stay around desperately trying to make racial integration work who are likely to pay the highest penalty.

If there were solid reasons to believe that racial integration would not destroy the value of their homes, a very substantial number, indeed the vast majority of Americans, I think, would not fear racial integration. Property value insurance schemes are both technically and legally possible, and there is considerable reason to believe that such insurance would be rather like the insurance of savings accounts; the mere fact of their existence would eliminate panic and make payments highly improbable. And yet the city planners and policy makers, as well as government officials, have never seriously investigated or experimented with the property value insurance concept. The mythology that people who leave racially changing neighborhoods are racist is so powerful that official liberal ideology requires that they be written off and indeed punished for their racism. Hence nothing has been done about the property value problem because almost by definition it does not exist. The cost of doing nothing about it, of course, is immense; it guarantees the outward movement from the city by the white population and the continuing profit taking by unscrupulous real estate operators.

4. *Crime.* Racial change today, like ethnic change in the past, has meant an increase in crime in the communities undergoing change. Civil authorities have not been able to control this increase, indeed, they have made no particular efforts to control it. Liberal ideology has long required that crime be attributed to poverty, and that those who are concerned about crime be written off as racists. This ideology has received a sound shaking in recent years, as liberals themselves have begun to fall victim to muggings in New York. (The ideology was never very strong in Chicago's "official" liberal neighborhood, Hyde Park.) It still manages to hold the fort behind the protection of security guards

in high-rise apartments in most cities and the protection of ever-vigilant police forces in the suburbs. What the liberal ideologues ignore all too often is that blacks are far more likely to be victims of crime than whites and that black concern about the crime problem is more intense than white concern. The fact is that no one really understands the dynamics of urban crime and no one knows what to do about it. However, much of the recent research would indicate that the old liberal explanations don't hold. Criminals in racially changing neighborhoods are not necessarily driven by poverty, they are not "protesting politically" through their antisocial behavior, they are not "victims of society" (though they quickly learn from their liberal allies the jargon of protest and victimization and use it freely). Some writers such as James Q. Wilson and Ernest Van den Haag have suggested recently that society's principal goal in dealing with criminals ought to be its own self-protection—a novel and revolutionary thought in our time. However, even if one is committed to such a theory, it is still not clear how effective self-protection would work. (One possible direction: it has been shown apparently that it is not the magnitude of punishment that deters crime but the certainty of it.)

In any event, no matter what the liberal ideologues in government and the press may say, crime is an acute problem in racially changing neighborhoods or in neighborhoods where the black middle class is being replaced by the proletariat created by welfare dependency. If preservation of the city is one of the goals for urban government (and given the fact that urban government frequently dumps the welfare poor onto defenseless neighborhoods, one would have reason to wonder whether this is a goal or not), then obviously strong measures must be taken to control crime in racially changing neighborhoods and racially changing schools. Such measures would certainly include flooding such neighborhoods with police protection and supporting and assisting neighborhood self-defense activities.

But self-defense activities, such as volunteer radio patrol cars, for example, are quickly denounced by the official liberals as "vigilantism" even when they are practiced by the black middle class (which has more to fear from street gangs and teenage toughs in high schools than does the white middle class). It is not "vigilantism," you see, to move across the city boundary into a suburb and thereby in effect hire a suburban police force to protect you from blacks who come from the city. Nor is it vigilantism to hire a private security guard to protect your own apartment building. But it is vigilantism for a group of people who live in an ethnic neighborhood to adopt self-defense tactics. A private, voluntary approach to social problems is a fine idea until it is done by ethnics, then it is by definition racist, because they are by definition racist. Racists have no right to self-defense.

Property value decline, fear of crime, and violence in the schools are the principal reasons for flight from racially changing neighborhoods. Racism—hatred of blacks—is also present and mixed inextricably with the other problems. Yet anyone who has lived in such a neighborhood knows that if financial panic and fear of violence could be eliminated, racism would turn out to be a relatively unimportant factor, and neighborhood integration would be easier to maintain. But note well that city policies do not merely fail to facilitate integration, they reinforce and strengthen the dynamics that make for the slow expansion of the black ghetto. It is almost as though urban government, urban planners, urban lawmakers, and urban administrators prefer the ghetto to racial integration. (Certainly some black politicians do, because they view the ghetto as their own political base.)

5. *Welfare programs.* No one in city government takes seriously any more responsibilities for anything but the "custody" of the welfare poor. It is generally realized, though not acknowledged, that the present welfare system creates dependency and imprisons the poor in the trap of their own poverty. It is also reasonably evident that the immense cost of welfare programs has played a substantial part in bankrupting urban finances around the country. The whole affair sounds like something out of Franz Kafka: you go bankrupt spending money on a program that only makes matters worse. But bureaucrats don't think of alternatives or even about helping people; they only think about administering programs. Part of administering programs involves hous-

ing the welfare poor, and one does that in the quickest and most efficient way possible by "dumping" the welfare victims on neighborhoods already threatened with racial change or by housing them in vast crime-generating, high-rise, ready-made slums which are not only dangerous for those who live in them but also for those who live within a mile radius, at least.

The welfare poor obviously are not being helped at all by being concentrated in one place. But it is more convenient to do that than to disperse them throughout the metropolitan area, just as it is more convenient to put up the high-rise slums (frequently destroying a perfectly good neighborhood to do it) than it is to build a thousand or two thousand scattered-site units. It is not necessarily cheaper to concentrate the poor into one place, but it is easier, particularly when effective dispersal of housing for the poor would require some poor people to live in the suburbs when the whole reason for the suburbs' existence is so their inhabitants can escape from the urban poor.

6. *Federal court integration policies.* The research of my colleague James Coleman has demonstrated beyond any reasonable doubt (though apparently not beyond vicious, irrational criticism) that the current policies of the federal courts to create racial integration are counterproductive and are forcing whites to move out of the cities into the suburban ring. The present volume is not the place to give the complexity of that argument, but it must be emphasized here that as long as the federal courts refuse to make racial integration a metropolitan issue, the results will inevitably be just what Coleman describes. If one can escape from busing and scatter-site public housing by simply moving out of the city, then most of those who can afford it will certainly do so. One scarcely needs research, only common sense, to realize that that would be the result of the compulsory integration provisions of the federal courts. If the judges were really serious about racial integration, they would mandate some form of metropolitan integration, which would mean integrating their own well-to-do suburbs, of course—hardly a likely result.

Yet it is very likely that some form of voluntary, subsidized quota integration of suburban schools, for example, could easily be facilitated with federal aid to schools being dependent upon the school district having a certain proportion of nonwhite students. Under such circumstances suburban school districts might vigorously recruit volunteer candidates for busing, as they now recruit basketball players. The movement of small groups of less affluent minorities into middle-class schools is precisely the situation in which there is most likely to be an educational payoff from integrated schools. However, such a sensible plan would not punish white ethnics and would threaten the purity of suburban liberal enclaves. Far better, Judge Garrity seems to think, to integrate South Boston than Newton, where he lives.

7. *"Disinvestment."* This is the most serious of the attacks on urban neighborhoods; its more popular, debureaucratized name is "redlining," a little-known process in which the banks and savings and loan institutions take money out of the neighborhoods and refuse to put it back in. In a careful study of "disinvestment," Arthur Naparstek and Gale Cincotta summarized the process in their booklet, *Urban Disinvestment: New Implications for Community Organization, Research and Public Policy.* Here are some excerpts from that booklet (pp. 9–10):

Phase I: *The Healthy Community*
The neighborhood is characterized by housing stock in excellent condition, by ready access to conventional mortgage money and home improvement loans, thriving local businesses, and good city services.

Phase II: *The Decision to Disinvest*
Pace-setting city-wide depository institutions and some local savings and loan associations set stringent loan requirements for that neighborhood, and indicate a preference for granting mortgages on new houses in the suburbs or other parts of the city.

Phase III: *Redlining*
Participating depositories determine to act more aggressively to channel money to other areas. The target neighborhood is "redlined," or formally selected for disinvestment. Mortgages there are offered only

under harsh terms (excessive down payments, higher interest rates, short loan life, etc.), or are refused outright. Institution officers justify their decisions to cut back on funding in the redlined area by claiming to perceive the risk of deterioration. Real estate appraisers, employed by the savings institutions, confirm the risk on the basis of subjective criteria. The analysis becomes a self-fulfilling prophecy. Loans cut off from the neighborhood insure that the housing stock will decline. Home repairs and improvements are left unattended. General confidence in the neighborhood is undermined. Potential buyers go elsewhere for loans, and find themselves steered to other, "safer" neighborhoods.

Phase IV: *The Rise of FHA Insured Mortgages*
Savings institutions concur in the decision to redline the neighborhood, and shortly conventional loans are considered to be "too risky." Inevitably, all the neighborhood properties are financed under FHA 100%-insured mortgages. Realtors, speculators, brokers, and big institutional investors, accustomed to the complexities of the FHA mortgage process, move in.

Phase V: *Decline*
The neighborhood is "turned over" in a few years. Property values decline, while taxes are higher, relative to the value of the properties. Absentee landlordism flourishes, and with it, the incentive for property maintenance disappears. Insured FHA mortgages compound the loss of incentive for property maintenance. Building abandonment increases. Crime increases. City services decline.

Phase VI: *Urban Renewal*
The redlined neighborhood is by now completely blighted. The city sells the property to well-connected developers, and large-scale, profitable projects are begun. Conventional financing reappears for the new developments, and the cycle is begun again.

Some of the redlining stories one reads about in the literature on the subject are absolutely incredible. Savings and loan institutions, having amassed vast sums of money from a neighborhood's inhabitants, physically move their buildings away from those neighborhoods and pour their money into other communities where quick and easy profits can be made without any consideration of responsibility to the neighborhood from which most of their money has been taken. Ninety per cent of the mortgage loans made by savings and loan associations in Washington D.C., for example, go into the Maryland and Virginia suburbs. Oak Park Federal Savings and Loan in the Chicago area made only $40,000 in conventional loans in Oak Park and made $1.5 million available to newer suburbs farther west. The story of one Oak Park resident who struggled with another Chicago savings and loan institution is detailed in the Cincotta-Naparstek report (p. 16):

> Another Oak Park resident, Bruce Samuels, went to Bell Federal Savings and Loan, in downtown Chicago, a billion dollar savings and loan, which 20 years ago actively solicited mortgage loans in Oak Park. The applicant, with good credit and an established job, was told by Bell Federal's staff that the house was "too old" for a conventional loan on standard terms. Yet this is a very solid, well-kept 55-year-old stucco-sided home. *We subsequently verified by the acknowledgement of Bell Federal that the Bell Federal refuses loans on any house over 15 to 25 years of age*—this is a billion dollar savings and loan—thus effectively boycotting almost all of Chicago and the established inner-ring suburbs around it.

The Chicago-based MAHA group, in a study of six downtown and ten neighborhood lending institutions discovered that three-quarters of the downtown loans and two-thirds of the neighborhood loans went outside the city of Chicago. Harris Trust (the financial base of the University of Chicago, incidentally) makes 97 per cent of its loans in the suburbs; Northern Trust makes 87 per cent of its loans there. The MAHA group also found that two-thirds of the savings and loan associations had simply ignored the Illinois state law requiring them to reveal zip code and census tract areas in which their loans were being made. Given the immense political power of the savings and loan institutions, such ignoring of state laws is probably to be taken for granted.

A friend of mine who is in the savings and loan business readily acknowledged that most lending institutions had redlined the entire city of Chicago, save for lakefront high-rise apartments. "We had no choice," he insisted. "The suburbs are just better places to invest, and we can't be the only institution investing in the city or inevitably we will begin to lose money and not attract savers. Only when the law forces everybody to invest in the city will there be a sharing of risks and no disproportionate losses for any of us." Thus while the savings and loan industry will vigorously oppose in the public forum any anti-redlining laws and will even resist fulfillment of their obligation under the mild disclosure laws, in private, individual members of the industry will express acquiescence and even hope that effective redlining legislation will be passed. It remains to be seen, however, whether neighborhood activist organizations like MAHA can amass the political clout to force effective legislation on the federal government.

Certainly Title 3, home-mortgage disclosure of the Federal Deposit Insurance Act, forced through in 1975 as the result of the national effort of neighborhood organizations is a step in the right direction, but such a step can only be effective if sophisticated research and analysis is done on the materials made public as a result of the act. (A group of my colleagues and I at the National Opinion Research Center are endeavoring to launch just such a research program.)

Regulations requiring reinvestment in urban communities are another solution to housing and racial problems in the city, which would benefit urban neighborhoods struggling to survive. "Affirmative marketing," vigorous campaigns to persuade people to move into old urban neighborhoods; commercial revitalization programs, the revival of business districts, which are the first to go when a neighborhood begins to deteriorate; neighborhood preservation projects; senior citizen housing programs; and single and multiple-family rehabilitation projects are all appropriate opportunities for reinvestment in city communities. However, it is clear that the financial industry will see such advantages only when they are motivated to do so by a combination of law and subsidy. That motivation need not require any additional costs to the federal or local governments, save for the cost of policing and enforcing new laws, perhaps. It probably would save government money in the long run because many urban problems would substantially diminish. The problem with reinvestment is neither technical nor economic; it is the problem of intelligence, will, and vision—and also, of course, the problem of greed among some moneylenders.

There is also a problem of narrow ideology and defective intelligence among those who think about, plan, administer, and police federal urban housing programs. Cincotta and Naparstek, in three powerful paragraphs, describe exactly what is going on (p. 38):

> A second conclusion of this report is that a crisis exists in our national urban policy. America's cities, the focus of the domestic programs of the 1960's, have been removed from center stage. The absence of urban rioting is taken by some to indicate urban health, when nothing could be further from the truth. Not only are our cities confronted with the same problems of a decade ago; they are now caught in a worsening economic bind as categorical problems give way to revenue sharing and block grants that often mean fewer resources for large cities.
>
> The Federal government is moving funds directly to states and cities with little concern as to how and for whom the money is utilized. On top of this, national economic problems have exacerbated the difficulties by reducing city income from local sources while simultaneously raising city costs. Cities have less money to spend, and at the same time, higher costs and little guidance on priorities. The result is that many human needs are going unmet. Moreover, economic necessity encourages lifeboat, or triage, strategies where certain urban sectors are written off as unsalvageable. While this may seem rational in economic terms, it ignores the attendant human tragedies and costs.
>
> Within the context of such a crisis in urban affairs, the neighborhood —the level of human interaction—has been disregarded by most Federal policies. The neighborhood focus, in political, programmatic and human terms, is not seen by domestic policy makers to be a critical focus. In fact, the persistent failure of programs directed toward reversing the decline of our cities is due to a tendency to perceive the problems on a grand scale, and a failure to define national policy initiatives and priorities which serve the varied needs of differing neighborhoods.

Various community organizations like MAHA and national groups like the National Center for Urban Ethnic Affairs and the National Training and Information Center are beginning to put together coalitions to bring pressure to bear on federal, state, and local governments. Yet the odds are stacked against such groups, because those who administer the federal programs, however liberal they may be in their ideologies, are in effect usually working in uneasy but close alliance with the panic peddlers, the blockbusters, and the mortgage industry. They share with the real estate and the mortgage profiteers the conviction that neighborhoods are irrelevant. Carla Hills, the former Secretary of Housing and Urban Development, came to Chicago in 1975, apparently expecting a royal welcome from local community groups. Instead she was greeted by a chorus of protests, and she responded to those who were paying her salary through their taxes by simply walking out of the discussion. All the MAHA group was demanding of her was that federal regulations be enforced.*

8. *Neighborhood abandonment.* This is one of the frequent consequences of the convergence of all seven of the previous problems. It is characteristic of the long, long delay between the two final phases of the model described by Cincotta and Naparstek. After a certain time, a neighborhood which has changed racially and has been redlined suffers the deterioration of its basically sound housing stock and begins to become a dumping ground for the welfare poor. Rehabilitation loans are not available, and the welfare poor are not very good at maintaining the apartments in which they live. The rigid urban tax

---

*An interesting sidelight on how the liberal intelligentsia thinks about such things was the coverage of the Hills-MAHA confrontation on television. Since the early 1960s journalists have been consistently sympathetic to protestors and demonstrators. However, one Chicago television channel turned completely against the MAHA protest and editorialized explicitly about the ugliness and futility of such confrontation strategy. I shook my head in disbelief, because it was one of the few times I have ever seen on television blacks, whites, and browns protesting *together.* There were Polish, Italian, black, and Latino faces on the same side of the table. Apparently protests are good unless black and white ethnics work together against the governmental and financial establishment—an establishment of which the television industry is a part, whatever liberal stance it may purport to take.

structures do not change, or at least they do not change rapidly enough to meet the new realities of the situation. The owners of the apartment building, having made a killing during the period of neighborhood change by charging high rents to newcomers, now find themselves only able to collect the rent allowances permitted by government welfare agencies. With such rental income, there is not enough money to justify maintenance, rehabilitation, or even the payment of taxes. So the owner simply abandons the building, and when the last of the renters moves out, the building stands empty—usually only for a short time, as it is soon gutted by fire—perhaps an accident, perhaps set by vandals or squatters, and sometimes set for the purpose of collecting on insurance. Eventually the city wrecking crews get around to demolishing it—at the rate of almost 10,000 buildings a year in Chicago. Sometimes even active neighborhood organizations demolish it, because an abandoned building is much more of a threat to a neighborhood struggling for survival than is a vacant lot. Such neighborhoods as Chicago's Woodlawn—once prosperous, then viable, and penultimately barely surviving—now have the appearance of Coventry or Berlin after the war—large tracts of rubble-strewn, leveled ground interspersed with not-yet-torn-down fire-gutted buildings. Not only the buildings have been abandoned but the neighborhood itself.

Frequently, as in the case of Chicago's Woodlawn, Oakland, and North Kenwood areas, the land is potentially valuable—near the lakeshore, close to good transportation, and within fifteen minutes of the heart of the city. But legal obstacles as well as the residual danger of crime in these neighborhoods (frequently very great) impedes, delays, and often prevents redevelopment. Even Julian Levi of the University of Chicago and the Chicago Planning Commission, one of the most sophisticated urban land experts in the country, has suggested (in despair, I suspect) that such areas will have to be "urban land banks" and lie "fallow" for up to twenty years.

Yet there is some irony in large tracts of inner-city land remaining undeveloped while substantial new land masses in the far suburbs open up for development—especially since the city desperately needs tax revenue and is unlikely to collect much from these urban land banks. Granted that neighborhoods should not be allowed to go the full route to abandonment, it is nonetheless true that many have already traversed that route and many more are far down the road. No one yet knows exactly what to do about such urban land banks; if we had a national urban redevelopment policy, highest priority would have been given to find the ways to make use of such almost priceless land. My own hunch is that the most serious obstacle to redevelopment is crime, or at least the fear of crime, by those who might possibly be interested in living and working in such redeveloped areas.

In the course of this chapter I have discussed eight different modifications of government programs which, with precious little increase in cost and probably long-run savings, would contribute substantially to the dissolution of housing problems in the city. They are: (1) tax credit–subsidized rehabilitation of existing housing stock; (2) metropolitan voluntary housing integration reinforced through the use of a tax deduction mechanism; (3) property value insurance; (4) assistance to local communities in developing self-protection programs; (5) dispersion of public housing and of the welfare poor until such time as a guaranteed family income can replace the welfare program; (6) metropolitan voluntary "integration" of schools as a substitute for forced busing confined to areas within the city limits; (7) effective requirements for mortgage institutions to reinvest in the communities from which they have drawn their savings deposits; and (8) a coherent development policy for empty land tracts within city limits.

While some of these programs might be technically more difficult to administer and implement than others, they are all feasible. If they do not exist now, the reason is not that they are too complicated or financially impossible but that liberal ideology and conservative greed combine to block them.

It is worth noting, incidentally, that none of these recommendations has anything to do with "celebrating" neighborhoods. While they would all benefit neighborhoods, they would do so indirectly by addressing themselves to urban housing and racial problems. One could, of course, take a further step and urge what Naparstek and Cincotta call a "comprehensive neighborhood impact policy." In their words:

> We need a *comprehensive neighborhood impact policy*—a policy which takes into account the diversity of neighborhood needs, builds incentives through appropriate local and state public actions, and supports the upgrading of public service delivery systems on the local and state level. . . . There is something wrong when there are no policies which prevent neighborhood decline without intervention until the point at which the process is complete, and urban renewal is declared. . . .
>
> We need longer-lasting, more fundamental actions and investments aimed at the neighborhoods. The "powerlessness" of the neighborhoods and their residents must change drastically if we are really talking about maintaining healthy neighborhoods—through joint efforts by citizens, city officials, and the private sector.

Such a "comprehensive neighborhood impact policy" would be desirable, of course. I think, though, that when dealing with most of the self-proclaimed liberals who are responsible for our housing and urban programs, that it would be politic to talk about "metropolitan housing and racial problems" rather than "neighborhood policies." The word "neighborhood" is a red flag that signals "blue-collar white-ethnic racists" to them.

I am not suggesting that urban housing and racial problems are simple; they are quite complicated. But I am suggesting that there are solutions to many of the most serious problems, at least partial solutions which could be implemented rather easily if the bias against neighborhoods and the hatred for neighborhood dwellers, which is so powerful within our national intellectual and cultural elites, could be surmounted, and if the unholy alliance between greedy conservatives and rigid intellectuals which dominates urban policymaking could be broken. The muscle of groups like MAHA is beginning to crack that line, but I fear that until many of our intellectuals and quasi-intellectuals are ready to reexamine their basic conceptions about human nature and the nature of urban life and take a good hard look at their anti-white ethnic prejudices, the nation's urban policy will continue to be a disaster turning into catastrophe—and a very expensive one at that.

Neighborhoods
Are Possible

And yet more kids . . . kids everywhere . . .
Irish . . . Lithuanian . . . black . . . Polish . . . Hispanic . . .
German . . . Slovak . . . Slovene . . . a few more Irish . . .
kids . . . kids . . . kids . . . loud, noisy, messy . . .
Ah, to have their openness to surprise again. . . .

A new riot has exploded in the city of Chicago—a riot of color. The citizens of Chicago have armed themselves with buckets of paint and converted the neighborhoods of their city into a carnival-colored fantasy world.

Get off the expressways or the main streets and choose at random almost any neighborhood within three miles of the Loop—Eckhart Park, Wicker Park, Pulaski Park, Bridgeport, Pilsen, Taylor Street, 29th and Wells, Oakley Boulevard, Logan Square, Washington Boulevard—and ride through the quiet, usually tree-lined streets. Bring your sunglasses and prepare to be dazzled, because the colors are overwhelming—blue, green, yellow, shocking pink, orange, brown, and at least a score of different varieties of red.

Is this still Chicago?

No one seems to be sure just how the color riot began. Apparently the Latins started it, and today the Latin area of Pilsen is the most ingeniously colorful neighborhood in the city. But blacks followed suit quickly; Washington Boulevard between Garfield Park and Union Park is probably the most gloriously colorful street in the world. White ethnics joined in the game, and now Bridgeport looks like the royal borough it is. Even such staid refuges as Beverly and Morgan Park are beginning to glow with roses and yellows.

The profusion of colorful facades has been made possible by the development of new one-coat house paints that can be applied to almost any surface. You can, if you wish, experiment with something new every year and never fear to run out of surprising hues.

But the color riot involves more than new paints. It is a genuine folk movement, as inexplicable as it is spontaneous and as delightful as it is unheralded. And when you immerse yourself in the sea of color, you will have another surprise: the houses themselves are beautiful. Until they explode in color, you never notice the cornices and the scrollwork, the window trim and the turrets, the porches and the bay windows. The painters force you to look at the details. Even the simple Chicago "cottage" has an elegance which is irresistible once you stop to look at it. The stonemasons, carpenters, and contractors who built such homes were interested in building durable but inexpensive dwellings for the hundreds of thousands of immigrants who poured into the city between the Great Fire and the First World War. And they were, it turns out, men of taste, imagination, and fantasy; the lines on their houses were elegant, the decorations fanciful, the styles crazy-quilt. "Balloon House," Tudor, Victorian, Greek revival they were—it didn't matter what fashion they were creating or imitating. These "architects" were folk artists in the literal sense of the word. They playfully, and at times wildly, did their work and then went on to try new tricks in each new neighborhood. They must have had a wonderful time.

Those who have painted these "ethnic" houses seem to have caught the spirit of fancifulness and exuberance of those who first built them. One generation of folk artists has been followed by another, no matter that ethnic lines have been crossed in the process. Pilsen was built by the Bohemians and painted by Latins; one need only drive through its multihued streets to discover that the painters knew exactly what the builders were up to.

Not so long ago, homeowners and neighborhoods competed in the display of elaborate, fanciful Christmas decorations. The competition died out when snow-covered streets of many neighborhoods became so crowded with "tourist" automobiles throughout the Christmas season that the residents could not enjoy their own efforts. Multicolored houses seem to have become the new Christmas decorations as the year-round celebration of pride in your home and pride in your community. If the man next door paints his house green, then you turn to pink or fuchsia. If Pilsen explodes in a skyrocket of colors, then Bridgeport will quickly fire its own pyrotechnics.

Why do they do it? The world has been created in technicolor, and there is no reason why the homes we live in should be drab, dull, and somber. Chicago's psychedelic homes celebrate their painter's joy at being alive and having a home to paint.

Many of the carnival-colored neighborhoods, however, are on the thin line between rehabilitation and abandonment, between a new lease on life and the wrecking ball. In most cases, I fear, the wrecking ball will win—it usually does. And that will be a shame. Much elegance and beauty and comfort, as well as color, will be lost—to be replaced by high rises, parking lots, expressways and vacant land. Buildings, of course, no matter how colorful, how beautiful, or how historic, can never be as important as people; and the preservation of neighborhoods cannot be more important than the successive human communities which inhabit them. But buildings and neighborhoods do more than just house the people and their community; they also reinforce and celebrate human ingenuity and community resources. A city which is careless with its homes and its neighborhoods really does not care about its people and its communities.

I suspect that most of the fanciful and fantastic homes I have photographed will not last more than a few years. Many of them are in districts where one can see decay creeping in at the edges. But in the finest Chicago tradition, they will at least go out in a blaze of glory.

But neighborhoods are essentially made up of people. The old man sitting on the park bench, the mother driving her children to a play practice, a teenager on the basketball court or the softball field, the toddler running off down the sidewalk, the old *babushka* trudging off to morning mass, the young woman walking to catch the streetcar, the bus, or the train in proud consciousness of her own beauty, the harassed teacher escaping from school at the end of the day, the "boys" at the bar, the "girls" in the coffee klatch, the elderly clergyman in back of the church, the college student glad to be home for vacation but ashamed to admit it—these are the people of the neighborhood, and it is for them the neighborhood exists. It is important not as a place, not as an object of nostalgia, not as a location of colorful names, not as a monument to relics of the past, not even ultimately as a guarantee of the variety and sophistication of urban life.

Neighborhoods are for people, and the only justification for having them is that they are good places for people to live—indeed better places for most of us to live than any available alternative in metropolitan life. The final justification for the neighborhood is that it is a guarantee and a protection for human freedom. Doubtless there can be narrowness and parochialism in neighborhoods—just as there can be in suburbs and university communities. The race tends to be narrow and parochial. The neighborhood at its best is ground on which to stand, a place from which to go forth and to which to return. It can also be, given human weakness, a place in which to hide. Still, in any decent and humane philosophy of life, society exists not for itself and not for the future or the past but for the individual persons who presently constitute it.

The social ethical vision on which this book is based stresses the organic, intimate, local, decentralized aspects of human life; but I do not believe that the organic network is a goal in itself. Rather that network exists to develop the freedom to protect the dignity and to facilitate the growth and development of the individual. If anything, the social ethic of this book—call it "subsidiarism," though that's a terrible name—is even more individualistic than that of the classical Manchester capitalism. It maintains, absolutely and irrevocably, that the dignity, worth, and value of the individual person is supreme and tolerates the subordination of the individual to no other goal. It defends an organic, intimate, decentralized social structure *only* because it believes that the dignity, the freedom, and the fulfillment of the individual person can be facilitated that way. It objects to socialism on the obvious grounds that socialism makes the state or the society the ultimate goal. But it objects equally to capitalist theory because for all its insistence on individualism, capitalism ultimately does not take the dignity, worth, and freedom of the individual seriously enough. Freedom of choice for the individual, for the family, for the small group, for the local community is not best served by viewing society as a battleground on which isolated individuals conflict. My philosophy views society as a network in which individuals compete and cooperate with one another with cooperation the dominant mode.

The neighborhood, then, is not a goal in itself any more than any other institution is. It exists for people. One defends the neighborhood because one sees no other form of organization of urban life in which the freedom, dignity, authenticity, and development of the individual, the family, the small group, the local community can be facilitated.

One can, of course, easily point to neighborhoods where none of these things happen; but the argument of this book is that neighborhoods are places where these things can happen, and are more likely to happen for most people than any other place in urban life. To say the same thing in different words, the nature of human nature is such that we spontaneously build neighborhoods wherever we can to the extent that conservative greed, liberal ideology, administrative incompetence, and impregnable social problems permit us to do so. The social, physical aspects of human nature are fundamentally unchanged —though perhaps greatly modified—by the scientific and technological revolutions of the past several centuries. Small groups and place are still essential for healthy and happy lives for most if not all of us. We invest ourselves in places and in local communities because there is a powerful urge in the structure of our beings to do so.

It is possible, of course, to be free without being part of a neighborhood, but only if there is some other community which provides us with security and psychological support. The frightened or lonely person finds it very difficult to be free; the anomic, isolated individual, at the mercy of urban change dynamics over which he has no control and about which he has little understanding, is not a free man. The principle of subsidiarity—no bigger than necessary—is fundamental precisely because it is a guarantee of personal freedom. The political control, physical security, and emotional strength that come from having roots in a neighborhood are essential for most urbanites to be free.

Here is the fundamental difference, perhaps, between the theorists of an organic, intimate, decentralized society and those of a mass society, be they capitalists or socialists, liberals or conservatives. We of the former group believe that freedom is ultimately facilitated by having roots, by having a place to call home, by having a group to which one belongs. They believe that freedom comes only if one cuts ties, deracinates and alienates oneself, belongs permanently and irrevocably to nowhere and no one. These beliefs are ultimately unarguable, because they are rooted in faith about the purpose of human existence, the nature of the world in which we live, and the design of human nature. But we, a curious combination of anarchist, New Left radical, black, white, and brown ethnics, are disciples of James Madison, Thomas Jefferson, and Catholic theorists; and we think that the burden of empirical evidence is heavily on our side of the argument. You can't be free without belonging, you can't be autonomous without being committed, you can't be independent without being secure, you can't go somewhere else unless you can go home again.

But for some Americans the argument about how best to facilitate freedom has become irrelevant. Freedom is in retreat around the world, and one by one the number of countries in which there is political choice is declining. The mass-society advocates argue that the complicated technical, and organizational problems that face a world of limited resources and increased means of self-destruction are such that we simply cannot afford to trust ordinary people with freedom. Such diverse commentators as Robert Heilbroner and George Lodge both see totalitarianism as inevitable, necessary, and, in Lodge's case, even desirable. The only question among such pessimists is how much totalitarianism will be required to protect the human race from destruction. Such pessimism, be it noted, is not really supported by any theological, economic, or political evidence. It is an act of faith, or perhaps unfaith.

The only way to run a metropolitan region, in the view of these pessimists, would be to give absolute power to the sophisticated Harvard-trained civil servants, who would sit not in City Hall any more but in Metropolitan Center and make the correct, wise, well-informed, professional decision, which would then be imposed and accepted either by the grateful consent of a subject people or by force. (In the Swedish model, such decisions are paid for by sophisticated bribery in the form of subsidies.) Under such a system one would have "the good life"; the allocation of resources and services would be fair and efficient, the people would be allowed to meet frequently in the local districts of such a region, much like the meetings in the collective farms of Russia and China, where one enthusiastically and unanimously endorses the goals and policies that come from the wise men in Metropolitan Center.

A brilliant new form of government? The future that works? George Lodge's New American Ideology? You might call it that.

Plato called it *The Republic,* and the only difference between his philosopher-kings who were to run his state and the Harvard-trained bureaucrats who would run ours is that Plato's were far better educated.

Some few of us, benighted no doubt, will be rather more inclined to choose Richard J. Daley's Chicago than John Lindsay's New York.

The slowly emerging national network of neighborhood organizations which are forming around MAHA and the National Center for Urban Ethnic Affairs is grimly determined to fight not only greedy bankers and real estate men on the one hand and the liberal ideologues and inept administrators on the other but also, if need be, the new totalitarians who are waiting down the pike with their benign smiles, their tranquilizing medicines, and their programs of "reinforcement" (provided perhaps by Professor B. F. Skinner, who is "beyond freedom and dignity"). One MAHA member remarked to me recently that the fight would take at least ten years. Perhaps it will take ten centuries. And a fair number of us may have to go out into the hills or down into the sewers, which we will if the programmers, the reinforcers, and the planners ever achieve power.

The future of the neighborhood does not look bright because in addition to all the present problems, the declining birth rate and the resultant decline in family formation will notably diminish the demand for housing in years ahead. There will not be funds available, according to some experts, for major urban reconstruction. The housing explosion of the last thirty years, in other words, will have come to an end; and we will be stuck with things pretty much as we have them now. And with urban processes pretty much as we have them now, neighborhoods will continue to decline and erode, suburbs will continue to appear (although more slowly), and housing will no longer be considered a major part of social policy concerns. The government support for reconstruction and rehabilitation of the city, as well as private propensity to invest in such efforts, will then flow to other areas of social concern. Even now, both funds for urban redevelopment programs and demand for the buildings to be produced by such redevelopment seem to have ebbed—though that may be a result of the economic recession of the early 1970s.

The economic future of the country is too obscure, as always, to accept easily such a pessimistic forecast, but one can find little grounds for cheery optimism either. If the emerging national coalition of neighborhood organizations have programmed a ten-year struggle, it may well turn out to be a struggle against increasingly difficult social and economic obstacles. To their credit, the neighborhood types realize that and shrug their shoulders with the comment that they will need even more muscle then.

And more faith. For while the ideas of localism, family choice, and decentralization are gaining supporters and while *Small Is Beautiful* has almost become a bestseller, the opposing faith still dominates the country's political, intellectual, social, and cultural elites. The neighborhood types are going to need muscle and faith merely to survive, much less to win.

But then muscle and faith were the secrets of those who built the neighborhoods.

Bibliography

Campbell, Donald T. "On the Conflicts Between Biological and Social Evolution and Between Psychology and Moral Tradition." *American Psychologist* 30 (December 1975):1103–1126.

Darroch, Gordon A. and William G. Marsten. "Social Class Basis of Ethnic Residential Segregation, the Canadian Case." *American Journal of Sociology* 77 (November 1971): 491–510.

Fanning, Charles. *Mr. Dooley and the Chicago Irish: An Anthology.* New York: Arno Press, 1976.

Guest, Abraham and James A. Weed. "Ethnic Residential Segregation: Patterns of Change." *American Journal of Sociology* 81 (March 1976): 1088–1111.

Heilbroner, Robert L. *An Inquiry into The Human Prospect.* New York: W. W. Norton, 1974.

Jensen, Richard. "Education and the Modernization of the Midwest" (mimeographed report). Chicago: Newberry Library.

Juster, F. Thomas. *Education, Income and Human Behavior.* New York: McGraw Hill, 1974.

Kantrowitz, Nathan. *Ethnic and Racial Segregation in the New York Metropolis.* New York: Praeger, 1971.

Lasch, Christopher. "The Family in History." *New York Review of Books,* vol. 22, no. 18 (October 13, 1975): 33–38.

———"The Emotions of Family Life." *NYR,* vol. 22, no. 19 (November 27, 1975): 37–42.

———"What the Doctor Ordered." *NYR,* vol. 22, no. 20 (December 11, 1975): 50–54.

Lodge, Geroge C. *The New American Ideology.* New York: Alfred A. Knopf, 1975.

Naparstek, Arthur J. and Gale Cincotta. *Urban Disinvestment: New Implications for Community Organization, Research and Public Policy.* Washington, D.C. and Chicago: A joint publication of the National Center for Urban Ethnic Affairs and the National Training and Information Center, not dated.

Nisbet, Robert. *The Sociological Tradition.* New York: Basic Books, 1967.

Schumacher, E. F. *Small Is Beautiful.* New York: Harper & Row, 1973.

Suttles, Gerald D. *The Social Construction of Communities.* Chicago: University of Chicago Press, 1972.